MY DENIVERSITY:
KNOWING DENISE
LEVERTOV

MY DENIVERSITY: KNOWING DENISE LEVERTOV

Mark Pawlak

MADHAT PRESS
CHESHIRE, MASSACHUSETTS

MadHat Press
MadHat Incorporated
PO Box 422, Cheshire, MA 01225

The Library of Congress has assigned
this edition a Control Number of
2021947557

ISBN 978-1-952335-30-3 (paperback)

Cover art and design by Marc Vincenz
Book design by MadHat Press

www.madhat-press.com

First Printing
Printed in the United States of America

For Richard and Nikolai, who were there, too.

Table of Contents

III. Journeyman

IV. Estrangement

"... James Laughlin met Ezra Pound in Rapallo, Italy, and was invited to attend the "Ezuversity"—Pound's term for the private tutoring he gave Laughlin over meals, on hikes, or whenever the master paused in his labors."

—The Poetry Foundation.org/archive

"[Denise Levertov] differed from other American poets in the high culture she had acquired in her home ... filled with books, [that] was the site of continual discussions about religion, philosophy, and literature."

—Czeslaw Milosz, *Milosz's ABC's*

Preface

My Deniversity spans almost three decades, starting when I first met—encountered—Denise Levertov and began to study poetry with her in 1969 as an undergraduate at the Massachusetts Institute of Technology (MIT), and ending with her death in 1997. But its principal focus is the 1970s, when she lived in the Boston area and taught at several universities here, and when she became my poetry mentor, friend, and confidante.

Denise arrived on the MIT campus a rising star of the post-war avant-garde, referred to as the "New American Poetry" after the 1960 anthology she and others appeared in with that title. She had already published seven poetry collections and a book of translations. Her eighth book of poems, *Relearning the Alphabet*, appeared in 1970. She would go on to publish an additional twelve poetry collections, another book of translations, a collection of short prose memoirs, and three collections of essays.

I've concentrated on the years when we lived in close proximity and spent considerable time in each other's company, the years when she wrote the poems that appeared in *To Stay Alive* (1971), *Footprints* (1972), *The Freeing of the Dust* (1975), and *Life in the Forest* (1978), and when she published her first essay collection, *The Poet in the World* (1973). Paul Lacey, in his afterword to *Denise Levertov Selected Poems*, described those years as the second of three large periods of her literary life, "when she was most overtly, but never exclusively, political in her writing, most torn by doubts about her poetic vision, given over to grief at the loss of her sister and her mother, and when her marriage end[ed]."

A physics major interested in poetry, not an aspiring poet, I couldn't anticipate when I signed up for her classes that knowing Denise Levertov would literally alter the direction of my life and career. *My Deniversity* describes the arc of that relationship and the changes I went through from curious novice, to poet acolyte, to protégé; from student, to friend and confidant, to estranged acquaintance.

Denise grew up in a suburb of London, the second daughter of a scholarly Jewish father who converted and became a minister in the Church of England, and to a Welsh schoolteacher mother who homeschooled her. As young woman after the Second World War, she traveled in Europe, where she met Mitchell Goodman, an American GI from Brooklyn. They married and settled in New York in 1948; their son Nikolai, their only child, was born the following year. They continued to live in Manhattan for the next thirty years, with extended sojourns as visiting writers to France, Mexico, California, and in summers to Western Maine, where they owned a farmhouse retreat.

In 1969, they relocated to the Boston area where Denise had a one-year writer-in-residence appointment at MIT, where I met her. They stayed in the area for the next several years, until their separation and eventual divorce. Mitch moved permanently into their Temple, Maine, farmhouse; Denise bought a house in the Boston suburb of Somerville and joined the faculty of Tufts University, where she remained until 1979. In 1987, she resettled in Seattle, where she lived until her death ten years later.

—Mark Pawlak, Cambridge, Massachusetts, 2021

MY DENIVERSITY

"You remember, Mark," Denise would say. "You were there."

I. Initiation

First Encounters of the Poetry Kind

"Whooo ... are ... you?"

In September 1969, my senior year at MIT, just before the start of fall-semester classes, I stood in the hallway outside Denise Levertov's office door in Building 14, Killian Hall, the humanities building, where I'd gone to submit to an interview in the hopes of gaining admission to the writing workshop she would be offering.

I had picked her class because of my budding interest in poetry and my curiosity about studying with a practicing artist. I didn't see myself as a poet then, nor did I aspire to become one; rather, I expected to go on to graduate school, get a PhD, and pursue a career as an experimental physicist.

I was feeling a bit anxious about encountering this exotic breed of person, the "practicing poet." I had only just learned a year or two earlier that not all poets were dead white men. Also, I had never had to pass muster before to gain admission to a class and I was without a clue as to how to conduct myself. I announced my presence with a knock.

"Mark Paw-lack?" she inquired, stressing the first syllable, speaking with a distinctly British accent.

"Yes."

"Come in. Come in. Pull up a chair." And once I was seated, "Tell me about yourself."

Ms. Levertov—"Call me Denise"—sat behind the desk in the otherwise bare office, where she had only recently taken up occupancy. A handful of books lay on a shelf on the wall beside her, giving the impression that they had just been hurriedly unpacked. The office was bare of pictures or decorations of any kind. Her back was to the room's one window, which opened to the grassy courtyard where Calder's sculpture *Great Sail* loomed.

She was dressed in a tight-fitting white jersey or sweater with horizontal black stripes, a dark-colored skirt and striped stockings. Her black hair was cropped short. I noticed right off the distinctive gap between her upper front teeth—"a sign of good fortune," she liked to tell people, I would later learn—and she was surrounded by a cloud of smoke. She chain-smoked, exhaling as she talked.

I was struck by her stature—small-boned, thin, almost petite—and by the sense of compressed energy like a coiled spring that she conveyed as she expounded. She didn't so much converse as dramatize what she was saying, her face animated, her hands gesticulating. She fairly bristled with electricity. I was entirely unprepared for the kind of vitality she exuded and a bit frightened by it. Hers was a presence the likes of which I'd never encountered. Barry Levine, another MIT student who became part of the same poetry class, told me years later, "Back then, Denise seemed more intense than any person I had ever met." It was a revelation, he said, that "someone could have that kind of life energy. It changed the way I looked at the world—to realize it was possible to be that way."

Sometime in April of 1969, near the end of my junior year, I had asked my college roommate for help in planning my final semesters of undergraduate studies at MIT. Joe was a physics major, too, but a year ahead of me. A mentor of sorts, he had offered me advice about many things and now I wanted his help one last time before he took his diploma and departed for graduate studies in England on a Marshall Fellowship.

My remaining physics courses were prescribed, but I had room each semester to choose two electives. Outside physics, Joe and I shared a common interest in folk music and literature. He was an example to me of how one could be serious about science and pursue art and literature as an avocation, too. A straight-A student, he also played guitar, and performed in coffee houses, singing folk standards along with his own compositions. He wrote poetry, too, served on the editorial board of MIT's student literary magazine, the *Tangent*, and was studying playwriting with Lillian Hellman, then writer-in-residence.

Joe knew that I wrote poems, having critiqued a few that I had the temerity to share with him, and so he offered, "Why don't you try to get into Denise Levertov's creative writing class? She'll be writer-in-residence next year." Until he made that suggestion, I had not taken my own poetry writing seriously enough to think of showing it to anyone other than him and my Boston University English major girlfriend, least of all to a professional writer, a real poet. Until he mentioned her name, I had never heard of Denise Levertov.

I had no idea what to expect when I had penciled my name on the sign-up sheet in the Humanities Office for the interview. I had never met a real poet face-to-face. The closest I'd come was when, with roommate Joe, I had attended a poetry reading by Allen Ginsberg to an overflow audience of hundreds at Harvard's Sanders Theater the previous year. It had impressed me as more of a counter-cultural happening than an artistic performance, Ginsberg, wild hair and beard, playing a harmonium and chanting as much as reciting poems. Excepting Ginsberg, Corso, and Ferlinghetti, I had had little exposure to contemporary poetry or poets. Of Levertov's work and reputation, I was entirely ignorant.

In advance of the interview, Denise had requested that each applicant submit a sheaf of sample poems, plus a brief written statement describing one's favorite poets and one's reasons for wishing to enroll in her poetry workshop. I don't recall whether she asked me that day to read aloud any of the poems I had submitted. I do, remember, however, that she plied me with questions, asking me to elaborate on the statement I had written.

"I see that you have a rather eclectic taste in English poets," she probed. "Blake, Wordsworth, Yeats, Graves, Eliot…?"

I confessed that until very recently, my exposure to poetry was through reading standard high-school anthologies. My interest in modern poetry, I explained, was sparked by two elective courses I had taken my junior year, one devoted to the collected works of Yeats, whose poetry I professed to like a lot; the other, to the poetry, plays, and prose of T. S. Eliot.

Denise misconstrued the mention of Yeats and Eliot together, as my thinking of Eliot as an English poet. "Growing up in London," she interjected, "I thought Eliot was British, too. It was only after I came to America and started to read contemporary American poets that I learned he was born and grew up in St. Louis and had attended Harvard."

Offering this personal note helped to put me at ease. Then, I told her my English-major girlfriend had read aloud to me poems by the British romantics Wordsworth, Byron and Shelley, and by such 19th-century American poets as Longfellow, Lowell, Emerson, Dickinson, and Poe; but that I had discovered Whitman on my own.

Denise chuckled when I related the story of my summer job back home, when I had worked on the maintenance crew of the Cheektowaga Town Hall. Most afternoons, I told her, the regular employees, who referred to themselves as "lifers," quit early and headed to a bar across the highway. I seldom joined them. Instead, I'd retire to the seclusion of a tool shed with my copy of *Leaves of Grass*, which I read cover to cover those sweltering afternoons. That same summer, I told her, I had also read Robert Frost's collected poems, sometimes with the book propped open on the steering wheel of the tractor as I mowed the town-hall lawns at a leisurely pace.

"Good choices, but what made you pick those two poets, in particular," she asked?

"Of all the poets we sampled in high school English, only Whitman's stirred me. I wanted to find out more about him, to read more of his poems."

"And Frost?"

"I took out a Book-of-the-Month Club subscription a few years ago, you know, just to broaden my reading. It was one of the selections."

At one point in the interview, Denise asked about my childhood: "Where did you grow up?"

"Buffalo," I answered, at which she crossed her arms and grasped her shoulders in the gesture of someone shivering from cold.

"Whenever I think of Buffalo," she said, "I recall the bitter, bitter cold and the wind-whipped, chest-deep snowdrifts." She told me that she had once visited my hometown to give a poetry reading at the university. What she remembered of that experience was that her ears and nose had nearly become frostbitten while she had scurried between buildings.

When the interview concluded, I retraced my steps through the battleship-gray "Infinite Corridor," connecting one MIT building to the next and the next, passing large stainless steel canisters of liquid nitrogen, resembling oversized milk bottles, and torpedo-shaped tubes of acetylene that stood sentinel beside the lab doorways. Outside once again, amid the world of trees, grass and sunlight; sailboats on the Charles River; joggers, strollers, loungers along the Esplanade; of auto, bus and truck traffic, I reviewed what had just taken place.

Halfway across the Mass. Ave. bridge spanning the river, headed back to my frat house in the Back Bay, I began to feel disheartened. Although Levertov had been very personable and had made every effort to put me at ease, I was convinced that I had made a poor impression.

My reaction to that first encounter with Denise Levertov is ironic given that I was daily in the presence of eminent scientists at MIT. More than once I had the occasion to discuss physics with Nobel Prize winners. They represented everything I aspired to become and more. To my mind, they were the epitome of scientific and philosophical thinking. But, although in awe of them, I nevertheless did not feel tongue-tied the way I inexplicably did during this one brief face-to-face meeting with the poet Denise Levertov.

She appeared to me in a dream that night: first, as Kali, the Hindu goddess of death and destruction; then, as the hookah-smoking caterpillar from *Alice in Wonderland* (the animated Disney movie version), blowing smoke rings out the gap between her teeth as she interrogated me, "Whooo ... are ... you?"

Imagine my surprise then, when a few days later I found my name included on the class list posted outside the Humanities Office. Denise couldn't have seen much promise in the poems I had given her. They were juvenilia, love poems addressed to my girlfriend, written in a dreamy nineteenth-century mode. Denise admitted as much to me about a year later in a letter she sent me in response to a batch of my new poems. She remarked then at how far my work had come, adding, "& you started at almost zero."

What had tipped the balance in favor of her admitting me to her poetry workshop was the lengthy term paper written for a contemporary literature course I had included along with the "required" submissions for her scrutiny. This paper had earned me my first A in humanities at MIT. It was a passionately argued comparison of Ginsberg's "Howl" and Whitman's "Song of Myself." In it, I had discussed Ginsberg's debt to Whitman, and compared "Howl" unfavorably to "Song of Myself."

"I found your reading of the two poems very insightful," Denise told me; "and your conclusion is right on the mark." She added, "Much as I value Ginsberg's work, I agree with you that Whitman is far the greater poet."

I looked forward to the start of her class with eager anticipation, curious about what it would be like to study with a working artist.

Contemporary Poetry

Having already studied Eliot and Yeats, two long-dead poets whose work was "meant for the ages" and having read on my own and enjoyed Whitman and Frost, I was curious to know what was happening in poetry now, beyond my limited knowledge of the Beats, and so, in addition to Levertov's poetry writing workshop, I also enrolled in Contemporary Poetry. No other elective course listing that semester sounded as appealing. It happened to be a course also taught by Denise, although that wasn't why I chose it.

Whereas the poetry workshop was intentionally small, a baker's dozen, to encourage the kind of intimacy and trust necessary when discussing one another's personal writing, Contemporary Poetry was three times as large and conducted in a more-or-less traditional lecture and discussion format with weekly assignments. In terms of the student makeup, there was little overlap between it and the poetry workshop.

Denise only occasionally assigned outside readings in the workshop, its focus being poems we students wrote and brought to class to be discussed. These consisting mostly of her own essays that had appeared in journals, which she Xeroxed and distributed (*The Poet in the World*, in which they were later collected, wouldn't see print for another four years).

Contemporary Poetry, in contrast, had a designated reading list that consisted of Donald Allen's *The New American Poetry: 1945–1960* and the then-newly published *Naked Poetry*, edited by Stephen Berg and Robert Mezey. These texts were meant to provide us a survey of the vital strands of current American poetry. Karl Shapiro's anthology of historical essays, *Prose Keys to Modern Poetry*, was included as recommended but not required reading. It offered some of the theoretical underpinnings of then-contemporary poetic practice.

Debates about free versus traditional verse, the finer distinctions between organic form, composition by field, and other open forms were very much alive and in flux when I first set foot in Levertov's classroom. There I was introduced to these ideas for the first time in all their varieties and shadings, including the ways that they were put into practice—or not—by living poets.

My science background didn't make it easy for me to wrap my mind around each poem or idea about poetry that I came across in the readings, but I did like the intellectual challenge they presented. According to Richard Feynman, one of my physicist heroes and a Nobel Prize winner, finding out how things work was "the real fun of life." I couldn't have agreed more. I applied that principle to all the high-school science projects I had undertaken. In each instance, with an obsessive zeal, I learned everything I possibly could about each of them. These teenage investigations led me to the realization that nearly everything can be interesting in a profoundly satisfying way if only you delve into it deeply enough—poetry and poetics for instance, especially when your guide is a practicing artist.

That's not to say I found contemporary poetry easy to grasp; quite the opposite. At first, I was intimidated by the many different approaches poets took to writing in open forms. The fact that there was no single right way to bring emotions, experiences, and observations together in a poem was unsettling. As a person used to the directness and certainty of scientific laws and mathematical proofs this was disconcerting. I was too new to poetry then to realize that doing science and writing poetry could share the common aesthetic experience of getting something "right"; i.e., constructing a theory or experiment, or making a poem that is both elegant and, as Einstein had said, "as simple as possible, but not simpler."

But my interest was piqued by the statements about contemporary poetics I encountered that echoed ideas borrowed from the Eastern religious philosophies, Buddhism especially. Reading Lao Tze, Gurdjieff, the Upanishads, Alan Watts, and D. T. Suzuki for a course I took in comparative religions had already acquainted me with these ideas popular on college campuses in the late 1960s. Indeed, I found that some of the statements about poetics were written in a quasi-mystical or philosophical language, and that others presented paradoxes not unlike Zen koans.

For example, Denise frequently quoted William Carlos Williams' phrase "no ideas but in things." But just what did that mean, I puzzled? Weren't ideas abstractions? What did it mean to be 'embodied' in a 'thing'? And, how could someone *not* have ideas, especially a student at the "Idea Factory," as MIT was often called? But at the same time, I worried that I was too much stuck on abstract ideas and lacked confidence about those things that spurred me to put pen to paper. Was I like the student Denise had admonished in her essay "Notebook Pages," when she said, "*The material of a poem must need to be a poem, not something else.*" Adding, "… certain material does not really depend on the *full resources* of language … but only on a kind of utilitarian recourse to language … in which case you should be prepared to write prose." I wondered whether I would I ever know for certain that what spurred me to write was the stuff of "real" poetry.

My persistence was eventually rewarded, but unraveling the mysteries of poetics as defined by those writers we studied in the Contemporary Poetry course was slow going at first. The concept of "negative capability," for one thing, which Denise, referring to Keats, discussed in an essay. This struck me as positively oxymoronic on the surface. I also puzzled long and hard over her statement that "form is never more than a revelation of content," and over her mantra, borrowed from Wordsworth, that, "Language is not the *dress* but the *incarnation* of thoughts."

I did notice echoes of Plato in her statement that "organic form … is based on an intuition of an order, a form beyond forms, in which forms partake, and of which man's creative works are analogies, resemblances, natural allegories." But whatever comfort I gained from that recognition was quickly undermined when I pondered those hard to pin down concepts of "inscape" and "instress," related but different, that Denise had adopted from Gerard Manley Hopkins and used whenever she discussed poems. ("Inscape being the 'inherent form' of experience

13

and 'instress,' the 'apperception of inscape.'") One moment I thought I understood what she meant by those terms, the next moment I felt they had slipped my grasp.

Statements by other poets in the anthologies we read were just as perplexing. Kenneth Patchen, for example, said, "There is such a thing as weight in words." He also wrote, "It is an absolute mistake to ladle out stress like a cook measuring off the ingredients for a cake." This, I presumed, must be poet-think, utilizing domestic metaphors to explain abstract concepts.

And what message was Robert Lowell trying to convey when he said, "The joy and strength of unscanned verse is that it can be as natural as conversation or prose, or can follow the rhythm of the ear that knows no measure." But then reversed himself, adding, "Yet often a poem only becomes a poem and worth writing because it has struggled with fixed meters and rhythms." And, then, reversed course again, stating, "... the glory of free verse is in those poems that would be thoroughly marred and would be inconceivable in meter." I couldn't decide whether he was for or against meter, an advocate or opponent of free verse.

Just as perplexing was Robert Bly's statement that "Talk of technique 'throws light' on poetry, but the last thing we need is light," which seemed to me not only contradictory but purposely so. Then he compounded this paradoxical statement by quoting St. John of the Cross, who said, 'If a man wants to be sure of his road, he must close his eyes and walk in the dark.'"

Occasionally, however, I did come across a statement that seemed to suggest some common ground shared by science, mathematics, and poetry. For example, the Keatsean formulation of beauty as truth and truth beauty resonated with my training in physics, which held that if a theory constructed to describe the universe was aesthetically pleasing in a mathematical sense, then it was likely to be true because the fundamental laws of nature *had* to be beautiful. I was reassured that I was onto something when I read Robert Duncan's essay "Towards an Open Universe." "This music of men's speech that has its verity in the music of the inner structure of Nature," he stated, "is clearly related to that beauty of mathematics that Schrödinger and Dirac feel relates to the beauty of the inner structure of the physical universe."

Several other passages helped me to make a bridge from the pursuit of one kind of knowledge to the other. For example, when Louis Zukofsky, borrowing the symbolic language of calculus, defined his poetics as "An integral / Lower limit speech / Upper limit song." I felt encouraged that poetry written today was something I could grasp after reading William Carlos Williams' definition of a poem as "a machine made of words." This suggested to me that the way a poem worked could be investigated in much the same way as dismantling and putting back together a pocket watch. As I read further, Dr. Williams went on to explain, "… it's not what [the poet] says that counts as a work of art, but what he makes with such intensity of perception that it lives with an intrinsic movement of its own to verify its authenticity." This view of the poet as *maker* and of poems as hand-crafted objects or mechanisms, each with internal workings uniquely engineered to suit their purpose, brought poetry into the conceptual world I was familiar with.

All these years later, it's impossible for me to parse which discussion took place in one of Levertov's classes and which in the other, but generally speaking, poetics and prosody, and the relation of theory to practice were topics addressed in Contemporary Poetry, while the focus of the poetry workshop was the actual making of poems that "had three legs and didn't wobble"—a phrase that Denise borrowed from Ezra Pound to describe a well-crafted poem.

Most of the time in both classes, I proceeded each day with a sense of intellectual vertigo. I didn't feel that I actually "understood" contemporary poetry or the theories that swirled around it—not, that is to say, in anything resembling the way that I understood relativity, thermodynamics, or quantum mechanics. Rather, I was going on instinct, "flying by the seat of my pants," lacking, as I was, the kind of navigational instruments I had acquired in all the preceding years I'd devoted to science and mathematics. However, I knew from studying physics—not an easy subject—that if I persisted in puzzling things out, no matter how complex or unfamiliar, the problematic knot would eventually unravel and I would achieve the "Ahah!" of comprehension. In

15

time, I began to recognize the topographical features of contemporary poetry and started to have some success in tacking from one landmark to another.

New American Poets

What made a lasting impression on me, more than the poems, statements, and essays, were guest visits by practicing poets Jerome Rothenberg, Jackson MacLow, Henry Braun, and Al Young that Denise had arranged. She also hosted public readings by Galway Kinnell, Gary Snyder, and Robert Creeley. As with the others, Creeley's was the first of many times in ensuing years that I heard him read his work. What I vividly recall about that event occurred during the Q & A after.

There was in the audience an MIT engineering student, no different from those of us present who were Denise's students, but unlike us, he professed to have no interest in poetry, or so he admitted to me when I talked to him later. He said he had just wandered into the room because the door was open and he saw the crowd inside. He had never experienced a poetry reading and so stayed to listen out of curiosity. Less than a year earlier that description would have fit me.

When Creeley concluded his reading, this student raised his hand and when called upon, asked him point blank, "Why do you read your poems in that halting, staccato way?" Creeley wasn't the least bit taken aback by the question. He replied that he read his poems just the way they were written on the page. He explained that his poems were made up of short lines consisting of just a couple of words, reflecting the way the poem struck his ear and that that was how he put it down on paper.

The engineering student looked no less perplexed after this explanation. Noticing this, Creeley invited him to come up to the podium and look at the typescript for himself. The student proceeded to the front of the room and while he was scanning one page, Creeley suggested, "Why don't you try reading that poem aloud for the audience." With hardly a moment's hesitation, the student did so, pausing at the line breaks and reproduced the cadence of Creeley's own recitation. That did the trick. He thanked Creeley and then went back to his seat satisfied, having learned something about modern verse.

Denise was charmed by the student's innocent curiosity and chutzpa. In the ensuing years, whenever she had occasion to lament a poet's lack of attention to craft, especially to line breaks—and there were many such occasions when I was present—she would recount this story. "You remember, Mark," she'd say. "You were there." Then Denise would not just retell, but reenact the story of Bob Creeley and the MIT engineering student, followed by an approving shake of her head and a hearty chuckle.

Wordsmiths in The Idea Factory:

Denise Levertov's MIT Poetry Workshop, 1969–70

My hope was that they would feel themselves, however ephemerally, a community of poets, and never as competitive aspirants for approval.

—Denise Levertov, introduction to "Poems from the MIT Poetry Workshop," *Hanging Loose* 12

We met one night each week for two and a half hours both semesters that year. There were about ten of us students in attendance at the first meeting. Over the course of the next few weeks, others joined the class until we had a full complement of thirteen. The assigned "classroom" was a black-box theater space on the second floor of the Humanities Building. Its track lighting, flat black walls, and absence of windows gave it a cave-like feel.

Denise instructed us to form a circle—some sat on stools, others on the floor, many lit up cigarettes. The atmosphere resembled that of a dimly lit coffeehouse, but minus the coffee, café tables, and folk music. Denise made some introductory remarks, then asked us each in turn to introduce ourselves. "Tell us what subject you are majoring in and about your interest in poetry," she instructed. "How long have you been writing? Which poets do you read?" Then, she asked each of us to read aloud one of our poems. After someone had finished reading, she asked the rest to comment, but if we hesitated to speak, then she took the lead and began to talk about what she thought were the strengths of the poem, in this way modeling how she wanted us to lead with positive feedback in responding to the work of our peers.

The first surprise was how many of the others were *not* MIT students: two were Radcliffe students; two, Harvard students; one a Simmons College undergrad; and one an oceanographer, ecology activist and recent graduate school dropout. MIT undergrads, half of them physics majors like myself, made up the rest of the original group; plus an electrical engineering major, a chemistry major, and a philosophy major. Others joined the class at later points in the semester or during the second semester: an engineering student at Northeastern University, a carpenter, who practiced yoga and Zen, joined for a time during the winter, as did one of Denise's former Berkeley students, who wanted to try out living on the east coast.

MIT and Wellesley College had begun an exchange program a year or two earlier, but this class was different, not a formal arrangement between schools, rather a decision Denise made on her own about who to admit. I suspect most of the other MIT students in the class came to it like me more out of curiosity about studying with an artist than a deep engagement with poetry. However, I viewed the "others" differently. They seemed to be passionately committed to writing poems; some aspired to become professional writers. Margo, one of the Radcliffe undergrads, for example, had a poem accepted that year for the groundbreaking anthology of women poets, *No More Masks*.

On the principle that she would always take part in the activities and exercises that she asked us students to do, Denise also read a poem of her own that first night, "Merritt Parkway." Heads nodded in recognition during her recitation; one or two piped up to say that it was a favorite poem of theirs. This, along with other remarks, indicated to me that many of the other students were already acquainted with, not just that poem, but with the body of her work. In contrast, poet and poem were new to me. I was embarrassed that I had neglected to follow my normally studious habits for class preparation. It hadn't occurred to me to seek out copies of her books in advance of the first meeting, although I did set out the very next day to purchase one. What I found between the covers of *O Taste and See*, my first Levertov acquisition, were poems unlike any my limited reading had prepared me for. Many were lyrics about common objects, actual events, and the rituals of everyday life, intensely observed, expressed in a sensual language that sometimes verged on the erotic.

I remember thinking to myself, after that first class, that I was venturing into foreign territory; also, that I was out of my league.

It seemed to me that the others were far better read and perfectly comfortable talking about poems, as if they shared a common vocabulary. Thanks to Denise's genial presence, these realizations didn't make me run for the door. I trusted in her command of the situation, which assured me that it was OK to be a novice. She had, after all, selected me to join this group for some reason. I remember thinking, "This could be interesting. There's a whole new world of things for me to learn here." Not a characteristic response for a seasoned MIT student, where intense competition with one's peers was the norm.

My prior classroom experience at MIT had, for the most part, consisted of attending lectures by prominent scientists, given in yawning halls that seated hundreds of students. I would try my best to listen attentively and comprehend what was being said, while at the same time madly scribbling notes to copy down for later study all the diagrams and mathematical symbols chalked on the blackboards. Room 10-250, the primary lecture hall, could accommodate my entire class of 1970, about 900 students. Because the MIT curriculum back then was very rigid, allowing for little individual choice, few electives, we all took the same courses our first couple of years; and so, along with my peers, I would take my place in that hall's raked seats that rose, front to back, row upon row the height of two floors. Humanities courses, with 20 or so students per class, were less formal. Professors, only one of whom was a woman in my six semesters prior to Denise's class, expounded on their subjects, invited debate, and moderated discussions of the texts; but seated at the front of the room, they were always the focal point of every exchange.

Denise's approach to teaching was in striking contrast to all this, as when she had instructed us that first night to sit in a circle and address one another. If we directed questions or comments at her, she would turn them back to our fellow students for responses. Her aim seemed to be to make us appreciate just how much we might learn from one another. Only after the last student had had her or his say, would she chime in—unless she was bursting with something she absolutely *had* to say, when she simply could not restrain herself. In this way, Denise let us know that we should view her as another member of the group—although, granted, the most worldly, experienced and, in terms of poetry, the most knowledgeable one of us, but not always the "authority" to be deferred to.

That first night, Denise laid down some ground rules, the principal ones being that we should listen attentively to one another's work and offer only constructive comments and suggestions. She made it clear that to honestly discuss one another's poems without inhibitions, we needed to respect and value each other's ideas, perceptions, and opinions. The charge she gave to us, which she herself modeled throughout the workshop, was first to say what we liked about any poem under discussion, to point out its strengths, the parts we thought worked, and only then to follow with suggestions about how the author might improve the parts that needed fixing—all of this was to be done in the spirit of 'mutual aid,' to which she subscribed, as outlined by the Russian anarchist, Prince Kropotkin. Whereas social Darwinists believed that the wealthy were wealthy because they were most fit to be so and that the poor were by nature suited to that status, Kropotkin disputed such claims. "[T]hose animals which acquire habits of mutual aid...," he wrote, "attain, in their respective classes, the highest development of intelligence and bodily organization." This aspect of her teaching philosophy was something very dear to Denise, as I learned over time, and not something she thought of as just restricted to the classroom. "Mutual aid" was a principle she believed one should live by.

With one or two exceptions, Denise did not give us assignments to be completed outside the classroom, between meetings. She had no expectations, she said, for us to produce a given number of poems or pages of writing from week to week. She treated us all from the start as if we were already poets, regardless of our quite varied experience as writers. It was her firmly held belief, she explained, that as poets we must have something to say before we put pen to paper. Poems, "true" poems, she told us time and again during the term of the workshop, must arise naturally—organically—out of the need we felt to express and give shape to our experiences, emotions, perceptions, ideas. Denise believed that classroom exercises of the kind, "write a villanelle," all too frequently resulted in artificial poems. She felt that if we had poems in us to write, then we would do so and bring them to class to be shared, read aloud, discussed.

Her manner was always personal, even intimate. Denise frequently shared with us her experiences as a creative artist in the belief that doing so would help us to recognize aspects of our own creativity. This included the possibility, she warned us, that we might go through what she referred to as "fallow periods" when poems just didn't come; but not to worry, she assured us, because it was a perfectly natural occurrence in the life of an artist. If it meant that for weeks at a time any of us did not have new poems to bring to class and share, then that was OK, she told us, so long as this didn't affect our commitment to the group and our ability to respond to the work of the others who *were* regularly presenting new poems. "My hope was not to teach anybody to write poetry," Denise had written about another poetry workshop she had led, her first, some five years earlier in New York, "... but to attempt to bring each one to a clearer sense of what his own voice and range might be and to give him some standards by which to evaluate his work." She made it clear to us that something very much along these same lines was her hope for our workshop, too.

On a night when there were only one or two new poems to discuss, Denise would devise an activity for us. I recall one early class when she asked Lucy, one of the Radcliffe women, whom she knew to have studied modern dance, to perform for us, improvising movements to a piece of recorded music, after which Denise had us all write down whatever came into our heads. Another time she asked Judy, the Simmons student, to play her flute as a stimulus to improvisational writing. She didn't expect that these activities would result in finished poems, she explained; rather, she hoped they might get our creative "juices" flowing in an unanticipated direction that, if we later returned to it and followed its course, might eventually result in a poem.

While most of these classroom activities struck me as things that Denise had thought up on the spur of the moment, others seemed more purposeful. One that she had us do early in the year laid a foundation of trust in one another for later sharing poems of a personal nature, especially ones that might reveal our vulnerabilities. "Paint a self-

23

portrait in words," she instructed. "Draw upon the plant, animal, or mineral world for metaphors that convey characteristics of your inner, private self." Afterward, we read aloud what we had written. Denise wrote alongside us and shared with us what she had produced. Notably, the only sample of this exercise that I preserved, in a folder of materials saved from that class, was Denise's own contribution.

Incomplete Monstrous Self-Portrait (in class)

Like the swan, I waddle clumsily on dry land—the dry land of certain relationships, certain situations. Or like a violently affectionate dog, I frighten some of those upon whom I rush, barking loudly, tearing their silken clothes with heavy paws. Yet in my own element I can glide strongly, regally even—yet less like the white swan than some waterbird of darker plumage that shines in colors. But I am a chameleon too, for among leaf-people I am a leaf, indeed a poplar leaf, never still; or among chair-people I am a chair, even an upholstered chair, and with rocking-chair people I rock well enough. (yet perhaps long ago my chameleon nature would have taken precedence in the constellation of selves—a pole-star that flickered!—while now it spends its days asleep under a stone.)

I can carry burdens from forest to sea sagaciously as the Thailand elephant, yet I beat on lit windows with the wistful passion of any moth.

(A slightly revised version of this was later anthologized in *Self-Portrait: Book People Picture Themselves*, ed. Burt Britton. Random House, 1976.)

This kind of activity, however, was the exception rather than the rule. Most days, there were poems to discuss, including Denise's own. These she brought to class either as newly finished pieces or as working drafts, poems that latter appeared in *To Stay Alive* and her collection *Footprints*. If we gave Denise our new poems far enough in advance of the class meeting, then she would have them Xeroxed so that everyone could have a copy when we gathered. Authors' names were always included. There was no attempt at anonymity, no false sense of objectivity when considering one another's work. "A poet," she would often say, "must stand beside his words." If, however, there wasn't time to make copies, then Denise would ask the author to read her or his poem aloud. Frequently, for the effect of hearing different voices deliver the same poem, she would ask another member of the class to read it aloud also, and then another and then another. There would be long thoughtful silences afterward, followed by animated discussion, in which we continued learning to address our responses *to* one another, not *through* Denise as mediator.

One of Denise's aims, it became clear to me over time, was to teach us to distinguish between mere self-expression, and "real" poetry, that is, poetry that draws upon personal experience but transmutes it through the writer's craft into art. As an object lesson, one night she read aloud a poem by Rod McKuen, who back then was the best selling "poet" in America. She followed it with a poem on the same subject by Yeats. Afterward, she sat back from the discussion and allowed us to name for ourselves the difference between concrete and abstract language, words chosen with precision to describe lived experiences versus generalizations.

I recall two occasions when she brought to class objects which she instructed us to observe and then compose the written equivalent of still-life paintings. One night, it was a potted plant; the other time a book of photographic portraits. Confessional poetry was ascendant in American poetry in those days. Robert Lowell was teaching down the avenue at Harvard, Anne Sexton was ensconced across the Charles at Boston University, and Sylvia Plath's collection *Ariel* was all the buzz. Counter to this trend, Denise stressed observation and objectivity.

Instead of the dominant *I, I, I* of so much of the poetry being written then, she encouraged us to use "objective correlatives," the term T. S. Eliot championed for using a situation or chain of events to symbolize and evoke in the reader a desired emotional response. As an example of what she meant by "objectivity," Denise read us Charles Reznikoff's paraphrase of a Chinese Sung Dynasty poet: "Poetry presents the Thing in order to convey the Feeling. It should be *precise* about the Thing and *reticent* about the Feeling." And, of course, she frequently cited W. C. Williams' mantra, "No ideas but in things."

The one formal assignment I distinctly recall that Denise *did* give us was to choose a poem written in a foreign language to translate, preferably, a language we spoke or had studied. The important thing, she stressed, was to pick a poem that had emotional resonance for us. She told us that she wasn't interested in the strict accuracy of our English rendering so much as in having us bring the essence of the original over into English, that is, to make an English poem based upon the foreign-language original. Since I had had four years of German in high school, I chose a short lyric by Goethe, *Natur Und Kunst*, "Nature and Art," which despite its brevity proved challenge enough to me.

This exercise, I later learned, was a standard part of Denise's poetry workshop repertoire, assigned intentionally as practice in the craft of poetry. She was still using it when, one day, five or six years later, we sat talking in her office at Tufts University, where, at her invitation, I had just made a guest appearance in her class as a "published poet." (It was Denise's habit to keep in touch with her former students; whom in many instances, became part of her circle of friends.) She told me that day that she continued to find this exercise useful. Her reasoning, she explained, was that student writers, undergraduates especially, because of their youth and lack of experience in the world, seldom had anything to say that was very original.

Denise then went on to qualify what she meant. It wasn't that she didn't respect the emotions and experiences of her students— quite the opposite. She valued their intelligence, perceptions, and the complexity of their feelings; but the feelings of young people are usually a muddle, she said. Added to that, as inexperienced writers, they hadn't yet acquired the language tools to convey their emotions clearly and accurately. Choosing a poem from another language, one that resonated with their own experiences, and then rendering it in English, was an opportunity for students to practice prosody without getting mixed up in their own subjective content since the original author supplies the content, readymade. "I almost always find," Denise added," that the outcome is a poem of greater technical accomplishment than anything the student has produced on her or his own."

Denise didn't provide us with a syllabus or any written instructions for this class; rather, she conveyed her expectations verbally. Just as there were few if any assignments of the kind write X number of poems, or produce Y number of pages by next week, or try your hand at a poem modeled on Z or write a sestina, so too, Denise assigned us no specific texts to read—unless I count Rilke's *Letters to a Young Poet*, which although not actually assigned, became the class "bible" because she referred to it so often, frequently quoting passages from it. In sum, her manner of instruction was what one might call the "inspiration" method.

She often read poems aloud to us by modern masters—Williams, Stevens, Yeats, Rilke in translation, as well as poems by her American contemporaries. Her choice on any given day was usually suggested to her by a topic we had discussed in class the previous week, or by one of our student poems that had been presented. Frequently, the poet or poem she picked as illustration was new to me. When that was the case, I would scribble a note to myself to seek out the poem by way of reflecting on and further absorbing the lesson. The attention we all paid to what she said and our eagerness to absorb what she offered, met, I think, her expectations for this class. We were all industrious, disciplined, self-directed—the kind of students that appealed to her. She told me once, years later, when consoling herself about the disappointing course evaluations she had received from students in the large Introduction to Literature class that she taught at Tufts: "I am best before an audience of students who are self-motivated and present because they are interested in what I have to say. Ones who don't need to be told what to do, but can think for themselves." Most, if not all of us, in the MIT workshop were just that. We were, as Judy (Katz-Levine) characterized herself at that time, "intense … about drinking in everything and absorbing all [Denise] said." The way Judy remembered it, Denise urged us "to write from the heart and to create intense moving work of high quality, consistently—emphasis on quality."

On more than one occasion, Denise read to us passages from letters or new poems written by one of the many poets with whom she regularly corresponded. I remember one such instance when it was both a letter and poem that Paul Blackburn had sent her. She read these aloud in their entirety then passed them around for us to look

27

over. On another occasion, Denise brought to class her copy of the journal *Origin* that she had just received. Published in it was a poem of her own—"Novella;" one that she had written the summer before. She used this as an occasion to talk about the importance to a poet of publication once one's writing had developed to the stage where it was ready to find an audience. She also talked about the role of small literary journals in encouraging and supporting writers.

The effect this manner of "instruction" had on me—and I know I was not alone—was to kindle a passion for poetry. Denise shared with us not only the associations that came to her mind of poets and poems both past and present, but also her own experience as a working poet. In doing so, she showed me that there was a living poetic tradition to which she belonged, one that existed in a spirit of camaraderie and of mutual encouragement among her closest contemporaries (another instance of "mutual aid"). She gave me an understanding of her vision of what it meant to be a poet. It had to do with being a craftsperson who belonged to a guild with something like Masonic or Rosicrucian overtones of mystery. By making us confidantes to dialogs with her contemporaries and by showing us her own freshly minted poems, Denise drew us in to the periphery of that band of poets, the guild chapter she belonged to that included Blackburn, Robert Duncan, Robert Creeley, Galway Kinnell, Muriel Rukeyser and Hayden Carruth, among others.

Although the poetry workshop had no required texts to speak of, Denise nevertheless handed out Xerox copies of two essays that she had published: "Some Notes on Organic Form" and "Notebook Pages." With these, she hoped to convey to us her ideas and convictions about poetry and her habits as a working poet. The publication of *The Poet in the World,* her collection of essays on poetry and poetics, among other things, was still several years off. When it did appear, I recall Denise expressing relief that her students would now have ready access to her essential ideas when they first crossed the threshold of her classroom. She said she felt that in future workshops she could expect a common base of understanding about her ideas on form, sound, and line breaks.

"Notebook Pages" included a letter she had written to a former student and subsequently copied into her notebook. This was the piece that I found most valuable at the time. In it she explained the distinction between what she called "poetry of ideas" and "true" poetry. It not only made a lot of sense, but it helped me see why some of my own poems didn't "work": they were all "head" and no "heart;" that is, they were just ideas and didn't incorporate my feelings, experiences, or observations.

Another lesson that Denise imparted to our class—and it came as a revelation to me—was how to read as a writer. From her I learned to pay attention to sound, shape, and structure in both prose and poetry. She would draw our attention to the way an idea was presented through the organization of sentences in a paragraph; to the comeliness of a sentence; to an evocative image; to the music of words in a poem and how their sound worked in concert with their meaning. She imparted, above all, the pleasure to be derived from savoring a well-wrought paragraph or stanza. All this she conveyed not through cold analytic dissection but through her enthusiasm for the felicitous parts of the text under study, an enthusiasm that was both genuine and inspiring.

Denise always privileged the "orality" of poems; that is, not just reading merely with the eye but also listening to the sound of each word as well as hearing the rhythm, tone and melody of a poem as a whole. Toward that end she would frequently ask one student after another to read the same poem aloud until every one of us had done so. Hearing the poem twelve or thirteen times in succession produced a deep intimacy with the text. The interplay of its words, images, and sounds, the way they all came together, gave me a new understanding of how the poem made meaning. Denise emphasized that we had to achieve that kind of understanding through "hearing" the poem, first, before we began to analyze the poem's components to find out how it achieved its effect.

The key to reading poetry aloud, she told us—and this was something she modeled for us many times—was to read slowly and clearly, articulating each word, filling one's mouth with its sound. If one of us started to recite a poem too rapidly, she would stop her or him and tell the reader to start again but more slowly this time—"feel the words on your tongue." Sound and sense, she told us, go together, they are inseparable in real poetry. To underscore this point she quoted on one occasion a statement from her notebooks by Pasternak: "The music of the word ... does not consist of euphony of vowels and consonants taken by themselves, but of the relationship between the meaning and the sound of the words."

However spontaneous her "lessons" often were, Denise was at the same time methodical in her effort to reproduce her own habits as a working poet whenever we gathered as a class. One way she did this was to share with us her practice of keeping a notebook as a way of "inviting the muse." Use your notebook, she told us, the way she did as a place to jot down lines from poems you find important to you, or passages that you have read and found to expand or deepen your understanding of what poetry is. If a word or phrase comes to you, or an image, write it down in your notebook, she said; also, snippets of conversation you might have overheard, as well as your observations of people and objects. Denise placed a lot of emphasis on the importance of dreams as a source for poems. Dreams, too, she told us, were worth recording in and of themselves; adding that once written down in your notebook they might also become the seeds from which poems sprouted. I recall that she once offered as example the fragment of one of her own dreams that she had recorded, which resulted in a poem ("The Broken Sandal"):

> Dreamed the thong of my sandal broke.
> Nothing to hold it to my foot
> How shall I walk?

After the poetry workshop's third or fourth meeting, Denise suggested a change of venue. Our Institute classroom just wasn't conducive to the kind of relaxed, intimate conversation Denise encouraged; for the remainder of the semester and the whole of the next one, we abandoned that black box to seek out more suitable places to meet.

One time, we gathered in a lounge in the MIT student center, where there were couches, stuffed chairs and wall-to-wall carpeting. Another time, we met outdoors in the old graveyard in Harvard Square. One weekend, Denise arranged for the class to travel together to the Cape Cod house of one of her friends so that, as a group, we might enjoy extended, uninterrupted time together and further bond. But mostly, we met in one another's apartments or dormitory rooms.

One class meeting that stands out took place in a basement apartment on Newbury Street in the Back Bay, on a block full of head shops, health-food stores, organic restaurants, and the like, long since replaced by expensive boutiques, art galleries, upscale antique stores, and pricey restaurants and cafés. Denise was unusually voluble and excited that night because she had just received an advance copy of *Relearning the Alphabet*, her new poetry collection, which she had brought along to show us. That evening turned into an impromptu celebration of her new book. The night concluded with her treating us to a private reading of selections from it. In the parlance of the times, I was blown away hearing Denise embody the persona of "A Tree Telling of Orpheus."

On several occasions, we gathered at the apartment Denise and her husband, Mitch Goodman, rented in East Boston. The final meeting of the yearlong poetry workshop was a potluck dinner that Denise hosted there. We congregated in her living room that night with platefuls of food and reflected on the months that lay behind us as a "community of poets." Denise announced at one point that she wanted to read aloud to us a long poem by Galway Kinnell, which she was very excited about. She told us that he had been sending her, piecemeal for comments, drafts of the poem as it evolved and that now he had sent her a complete final draft to review and critique.

We were all quite familiar with Kinnell's poetry. Many of us had the sound of his voice declaiming poems in our heads from the reading he'd given on campus earlier in the year. I had all but committed to memory several of poems from his last book, *Body Rags*, and I thought of his "Avenue C" poem as a masterpiece. I remember feeling a kind of conspiratorial excitement at sharing in the intimacy between these two masters of the poet's craft. We listened rapt that night as Denise read *A Book of Nightmares* in its entirety without pause. After a long meditative silence one or two spoke. We were all left in awe of its scope and the richness of its language and imagery.

That evening brought closure to our "class;" but it had greater significance of a ritualistic kind for me, and, I suspect, for many of the others, too. I think that, for Denise, it represented the culmination of her ambitions as a teacher of poetry, which she reflected upon in "The Untaught Teacher," the essay she was writing at the time:

> "... [to] generate, and ferment among the students, enough passion and drama to produce a *collective* epiphany; and this not for its own sake ... so much as for the sake of its function as gateway, portal, to new levels of feeling, to a greater openness after passing through it, and the sense of comradeship than can develop even among quite a large number of people who have been together in a time of crisis or revelation."

Although I still had many years ahead of me in my poetry apprenticeship, I left Denise's apartment that night and walked back to the T station feeling that I was no longer just a student of poetry, but that I was now an initiate into the fellowship of poets.

Praxis

Tin soldiers and Nixon coming …
—Neil Young, "Ohio"

One of Denise's guiding principles I quickly learned was her belief that if as an artist your life was whole and not compartmentalized—as hers certainly was not—then it was inconceivable to share your work—poems in her case—both on the page and in public forums, without also sharing your convictions, especially in such troubled times when America's urban ghettos were burning and an unpopular war was being waged overseas in Vietnam. From early on in her career as poet/activist, she viewed invitations to read her poems as opportunities to educate audiences about social injustice and the immorality of the Vietnam War and to persuade them to join in social action and resistance to the war's continuation.

One such occasion took place in January 1970, just as the final semester of our poetry workshop was beginning. Boston that year was a hotbed of draft resistance and antiwar protests with an office in Cambridge staffed by student activists from campuses on both sides of the Charles coordinating "actions" across the entire greater Boston area. It was command central for rallies and demonstrations on the Boston Common as well as at Harvard, MIT, Boston University, and Northeastern, among other schools. Each protest or disruption of the status quo planned for one campus drew student radicals from the others, joining their comrades in what they viewed to be acts of revolutionary solidarity.

"Northeastern Conspiracy—A Call to Action" read the fliers handed out on street corners, stapled to telephone poles, tacked to bulletin boards, and pasted on walls across the city that January. I don't recall now just what the "conspiracy" was thought to be, if I ever knew, but I remember that the plan was for three days of demonstrations against the visit to the Northeastern University campus by General Electric job recruiters—GE being a notorious defense contractor. The culminating event would be a January 29th rally to protest the talk by San Francisco State University President S. I. Hayakawa scheduled to be delivered as part of Northeastern's distinguished lecturers series.

Hayakawa was a lightning rod, attracting student protesters wherever he appeared, in no small part because he had been widely praised by the likes of President Nixon, Nixon's oratorical hatchet-man, Vice President Spiro Agnew, and California governor Ronald Reagan for "standing up" to students. They held Hayakawa up as a model for college administrators nationally after his refusal to negotiate with student agitators and their faculty supporters at San Francisco State. Instead he had closed the campus for several months, locking students and faculty out, refusing to give their complaints a hearing. Attempts to rally opposition to his decision were met by ranks of San Francisco police and National Guardsmen, mobilized by Hayakawa and Reagan. Photographs of protesters brutally beaten were widely circulated through the underground presses at the time.

But that same January evening, Denise was scheduled to read her poems as a fundraiser for Ecology Action. The venue was the meeting hall of the Old Cambridge Baptist Church (OCBC) in Harvard Square, the basement of which was a warren of office cubicles given over to activist groups of every cause and persuasion. Denise felt obliged to keep this commitment, despite her ardent desire to take part in the demonstration against Hayakawa. ("You remember, Mark, you were there.")

Fellow poetry workshop student Margo and I had arranged to meet Denise at the Harvard subway station and accompany her on the short walk to the church. Listening to her agonize about her inability to be in both places at the same time, we hatched a plan to mollify her disappointment. It went like this: Margo and I would leave Denise off at the church to read her poems while we proceeded across the river to the Northeastern demo. We would periodically report back what was happening there via pay phone to a designated church staffer, who would pass our messages to Denise; and Denise, in turn, would inform the audience. According to this scenario, after her reading, if our reports indicated that the demo still had life to it, Denise, and anyone in attendance she could enlist to accompany her, would cross the river and add their voices to the protest against Hayakawa.

Margo and I were confident that Denise would draw connections for her audience between the corporate power structure that was responsible for policies resulting in destruction of the environment and Hayakawa, who advocated support for the status quo, including the war in Vietnam. Knowing her powers of persuasion, we were also confident that she would be able to recruit some of the attendees to follow her lead and cross the river to join the demonstration.

Margo and I caught The People's Bus, a van that at the time conveyed hitchhikers free of charge along the central artery, Massachusetts Avenue, across the Charles to where it intersected Huntington Avenue in Boston. Disembarking there, we found a pitched battle already in progress: sirens wailing, police in riot gear, acrid clouds of tear gas in the air.

As it happens, Huntington Ave. passes under Mass. Ave. by way of a tunnel. Where Huntington re-emerges there is a physical barrier dividing the street down the middle, separating northbound from southbound surface traffic. We joined a seesaw battle between police and demonstrators that was taking place on either side of the brick-walled tunnel exit and the wrought iron fencing that borders the subway tracks. A phalanx of police, using shields and truncheons, pushed the mass of protesters back down one side of Huntington, only to find us running around to the other side of the barrier, trying to outflank them and gain access to the Northeastern campus grounds behind. Over the fray, a block or two beyond, I could see students clashing with police, others chased, running, some being clubbed, still others dragged to waiting paddy wagons. Newspaper reports later revealed that in the fracas that night, police had arrested not only protesters but any college-age male they encountered, including innocents coming from evening classes or from studying in the library.

Margo and I twice left the skirmish to find a pay phone and report what we had observed to the OCBC staffer. "It's a police riot. Bring as many people as you can round up," was our last message for Denise back in Harvard Square, shouted into the telephone over the din. The battle raged on, but our contingent on Mass. Ave. was unable to outflank or break through the police lines. All the while, Margo and I kept an eye out for Denise, fully expecting her at any moment to step off the People's Bus and tap us on the shoulder.

But the plan we'd hatched had a fatal flaw. We had forgotten that there were multiple ways to travel from Harvard Square to Northeastern University. The Arborway branch of the Green Line subway, for one. It emerges from underground at the Huntington/Mass. Ave. intersection, then continues on the surface with a stop at Northeastern University. Half an hour after our last phone report, we saw, to our shock and horror, over the heads of the police, at the point where the subway disgorged passengers at the Northeastern stop, Denise emerging from one Green Line car into the midst of the melee, followed by half a dozen young men.

They were immediately surrounded by police; the young men clubbed, cuffed, and dragged away to waiting vans. Although we could not hear what she was shouting, we could make out Denise's figure through the clouds of gas, her arms flailing, shouting at the riot police as she followed behind her young comrades.

Our contingent was eventually pushed back onto Mass Ave when police renforcements arrived and then dispersed with tear gas. There was no way we could reach Denise. All other avenues of access to the campus were blocked, so Margo and I returned to Cambridge. Meeting up the next day, Denise told us that she was never arrested, no doubt because of her age and professional attire, but had spent the night in the jailhouse, helping to arrange bail for those who were.

In the ensuing days, I learned details from friends who had been inside the auditorium about how they and fellow radical students had succeeded in planting themselves in the audience despite screening at the entrance by campus security personnel and had disrupted Hayakawa's talk, shouting "Warmonger" and "Fascist!" Most were dragged off by police and some severely beaten. Outside the auditorium, their supporters clashed with squads of police, resulting in the skirmishes that we had witnessed from a distance.

Denise's social justice advocacy and opposition to the Vietnam War were, however, not always greeted with approval or listened to with deference by those attending her poetry readings. Fast forward to May 8, 1970, almost five months after the Hayakawa demonstration and just one month after four students were shot dead by National Guardsmen at Kent State during an anti-war protest. I wasn't present at Goucher College in Maryland, where a chapel service was held in the dead students' memory to which Denise had been invited as participant, but she later documented what occurred in a poem.

"The Day the Audience Walked Out on Me, and Why," describes how, after she read two of her best-known Vietnam poems, "Life at War" and "What They Were Like," she told those seated in the chapel, addressing the fact that all four of the Kent State students were white,

> ... let us be sure we know
> our gathering is a mockery unless
> we remember also
> the black students shot at Orangeburg two years ago,
> and Fred Hampton murdered in his bed
> by the police only months ago.

According to the poem, as she continued speaking in this vein, "girls, older women, men," began to stand up, turned their backs to the altar and walked out.

> By then the pews were almost empty
> and I returned to my seat and a man stood up
> in the back of the quiet chapel
> ....
> and said my words
> desecrated a holy place.

Denise concluded her poem with these lines:

And a few days later
when some more students (black) were shot
at Jackson, Mississippi,
no one desecrated the white folks' chapel,
because no memorial was held.

II. Apprenticeship

Sketches of Denise Levertov and Mitchell Goodman

We do not remember days, we remember moments.
—Cesare Pavese

Mitch

I first met Denise's husband Mitchell (Mitch) Goodman in the fall of 1969 when the MIT poetry class gathered at their Webster Street apartment in East Boston. Tall, lanky, balding and self-absorbed, Mitch was a shadowy presence, rummaging in other rooms and passing through where we students sat on his way upstairs. He showed little interest in talk, although he may have just been following Denise's instructions to stay out of the way so that she could conduct her class.

I had an altogether different impression of him when a few weeks later he turned up with Denise at another class meeting, this time at a fellow student's Cambridge apartment. That evening started out with a potluck dinner. We sampled food, drank wine, listened to music, talked, and smoked a lot of cigarettes—something we all did at the time. A joint was passed around and then poems were read aloud. When it came to be Mitch's turn to share, he drew himself up, grew serious. He wished to use the occasion, he told us, to remember the life and legacy of Jack Kerouac, who had died the previous week.

Mitch spoke in a commanding manner about the importance of Kerouac as both writer and countercultural pioneer, who documented the lives and exploits of the Beats; but Mitch also lamented Kerouac's descent into alcoholism and drug abuse, which resulted in his death. Then Mitch read a lengthy passage from *On the Road*, pausing from time to time to extol the rhythmic language of Kerouac's prose, which he clearly admired.

I don't recall whether Mitch read any of his own poems that night, although Denise revealed that he did occasionally write poems. I do remember that he spoke at length about the importance and influence of William Carlos Williams, who was as dear to him as to Denise. If not that night, then on another occasion, he praised not just Doc Williams' poems, but also his stories, novel, and essays, recommending especially that we read *In the American Grain*.

Denise and Mitch both spoke of certain people in tones approaching reverence: in addition to Williams, Pound (with the usual political misgivings), Olsen, H. D. ... and in the political realm, A. J. Muste, David Dellinger, and Barbara Deming. Paul Goodman was another. Denise admired his poem "The Lordly Hudson"; Mitch considered him a major cultural critic and political thinker, and he liked to think of himself as cast in the same mold and strove to attain a comparable stature among his New York literary intellectual peers.

Mitch's style was to make pronouncements with a Brooklyn street tough's bravado about anything and everything: the greatness of William Carlos Williams, the significance of the latest government policy shift in the Vietnam War, the best rye bread on the East Coast, etc. His utterances were a challenge to anyone within earshot to dare contradict him. They were also, I learned over time, a defense against his insecurity and low self-esteem in Denise's company.

Mitch was on probation when I first met him, a sentencing condition of his federal conspiracy trial for counseling young men to resist the Selective Service draft. Mitch, along with his co-defendants Dr. Benjamin Spock, Rev. William Sloane Coffin, Marcus Raskin and William Ferber, The Boston Five, were front-page news in 1968, mostly because Dr. Spock, "America's baby doctor," was risking jail to publicly voice his opposition to the war. Their convictions were later overturned, but when I first knew him, Mitch was still under threat of being retried and so was laying low, no longer organizing anti-war rallies or leading marches. He had to content himself with being one of the crowd. As a result, Denise stepped forward and took on a more publicly visible role.

There was seldom a conversation where Mitch and Denise were involved that did not mention "The Movement." They always spoke of "The Movement," rarely of the "counterculture" or the "New Left." Their conception of it was inclusive, stretching from the '50s anti-bomb rallies and civil rights marches to draft resistance, anti-war activism, SDS, Weatherman, the Black Power Movement, the Women's Movement (at first called Female Liberation), and Gay Liberation. Sectarianism was antithetical to their thinking.

Mitch had primarily supported himself with journalism, writing travel pieces for newspapers and magazines. In the early '60s, he had published *The End of It*, an anti-war novel that was praised by Norman Mailer, among others; but when I first met him and for several years afterward, he was occupied with gathering material for his compendium of "The Movement." Published by Beacon Press, it was testimony to the inclusiveness he and Denise believed in. At 750 pages, it rivaled the Manhattan Yellow Pages in size, and had a title commensurate with its length: *The Movement Toward A New America: The Beginning of a Long Revolution*.

In the winter of 1969–1970, during the year I studied with Denise, radical students protesting Defense Department funding of military research on campus had stormed MIT President Howard Johnson's offices. Many MIT faculty gave verbal support to their occupation, but Denise was the only one to stay through the night with the students as "protection" against police violence in the event of an early morning "bust." I went inside several times during the occupation to show support for the group, which included some of my friends, passing through the intimidating gauntlet of campus police and undercover cops taking pictures. At one point, I found Denise in a corner of the crowded room, holding a copy of *Catch 22*. She was about to return it to the president's bookshelf from where she had "borrowed" it the day before. In an intimate moment, she revealed that Heller's novel had appeared at the same time as Mitch's anti-war novel, but it had stolen all the attention—unfairly, she had always felt. "Out of loyalty to Mitch, I had never read *Catch 22* until last night," she confessed. Now that she finally had, she admitted, it was "pretty good."

43

My impression, listening to Mitch and Denise talk, was that they knew everyone who was anyone, coast to coast, or especially everyone on East and West coasts. They viewed the great midlands as "populated" by islands of activists, primarily on college campuses—all of whom they were also acquainted with. Mitch often described himself as "a charter member of the great conspiracy on behalf of 'The Movement,'" as indeed he was.

In those days, WBCN, the Boston FM rock station we all listened to, had Danny Schechter as its self-styled "news dissector." Dissecting the news—print, radio, and TV—was something we had all learned to do to uncover the truth about the conduct of the war and learn about the rebellion in the streets of American cities. Mitch was a master at this. It was his ritual to take apart and reconstruct the daily *New York Times* and *Washington Post* coverage and report his findings to whoever was within earshot.

Viewing *I. F. Stone's Weekly*, the documentary film made in the early '70s about the legendary independent journalist, I remember thinking it was the correlative for Mitch's mind at work on the news. In the film, Izzy Stone is shown riding around Washington in the backseats of cabs reading a pile of daily newspapers. He neatly tears out news items, saving them to be later reassembled in his weekly *Report*. (Stone once sarcastically quipped that the *Washington Post* was an exciting newspaper to read, "because you never know on what page you will find a page one story.")

Brook Street

After graduating from MIT, I took a job teaching in an experimental "free" school in Santa Barbara. At the end of that year on the West Coast, I returned to Boston, in large part because I missed the intellectual stimulation. Alumni of Denise's MIT poetry workshop still residing in the area were among the first people I looked up—and Denise herself, of course. I learned that she and Mitch had moved in the interim from East Boston to Brookline Village, where they shared a large house in a communal arrangement with two other couples. When I rang the bell at the spacious Victorian on Brook Street, Denise answered the door, greeting me with open arms—literally. We talked for hours it seemed, catching one another up on our recent travels, current doings, and our plans. We also traded news about the whereabouts and activities of the other members of the MIT poetry workshop, and, as always, we each shared new poems.

I knew Denise hadn't been rehired by MIT because of her political involvement with campus student protests, including the occupation of the President's Office, but I didn't know she had worried she wouldn't be able to find another teaching job. To her relief, she told me, Kirkland College, a small liberal arts women's college in upstate New York, hired her as writer-in-residence during the year I was away. Grateful as she was to be employed, she admitted during my visit that it had wearied her to travel there weekly. Situated in a small town between Albany and Syracuse, it was almost a five-hour car ride, but since she didn't drive, it took her even longer to get there by bus. I reminded her I was well acquainted with the route, having traveled it between Boston and my hometown, Buffalo, for school holidays while an undergrad. Recounting the sudden winter blizzards, we could laugh in retrospect about the frequently snarled traffic along the Interstate and the spontaneous communities of travelers waiting out the storms at rest stops.

That day, I brought up the subject of "Staying Alive," the book-length poem she had begun to write a year or two prior to arriving in Boston. Her "notebook poem" was how she always referred to it, feeling that the loose journal form was best suited to the task of working through the tensions between her antiwar activism and her poetic vocation. The critical response to its eventual publication was starkly divided. Some of her former poetry admirers accused her of abandoning lyricism for a hectoring didacticism.

Denise had continued to add to the notebook poem during the year she taught at MIT, sharing with us students those parts she was composing then. During the year I was in Santa Barbara, she had mailed to me a draft of its final section, written after I had left for the West Coast. Although I was very much a novice poet, she always made me feel she valued my opinion. Now, seeing her in person, I was eager to make up for what I felt had been an inadequate, half-formed, response to the draft.

That first visit back, or in a subsequent one, I let Denise know I hoped to "apprentice" myself to her to better master the craft of poetry. What better way, I thought, to test whether I had it in me to become a real poet, to answer for myself the question that Rilke posed in *Letters to A Young Poet*: "*Must* I write?" Denise, of course, welcomed my intentions.

During another visit to Brook Street, I told her I had begun to volunteer at The Group School, which was just getting started in Cambridge. She seemed genuinely pleased to learn I hadn't given up on teaching in alternative settings. Unlike the upper-middle-class clientele of the Santa Barbara Free School, The Group School enrolled disaffected poor and working-class Cambridge teens, many of whom lived in public housing and many of whom had been chronically truant or had dropped out of their public high school altogether.

Mitch was also excited to learn about my involvement with The Group School, especially when I described its philosophy of participatory democracy in which students together with teachers, after long drawn out discussions, made decisions by consensus about admissions, discipline, and even curriculum. He reminded me that their friend George Dennison, had been instrumental in starting the First Street School in Manhattan, which led him to write his best-seller, *The Lives of Children,* a seminal text of the "free school" movement. Dennison, Mitch told me, had since relocated to Maine as their neighbor in Temple.

My first year back in Boston I was unsettled, sleeping on friends' couches until I wore out my welcome, then I rented rooms in a succession of boarding houses and crash pads, until I was invited to move into the Cambridge Centre Street collective with Richard Edelman and his activist comrades. Richard, like me, was an alum of Denise's MIT poetry class. He and others in that shared apartment had recently started The Hovey Street Press, a radical printing collective that published handbills, fliers, posters and pamphlets for The Movement.

We lived hand to mouth at Centre Street. The press had a hard time paying for paper and ink, let alone a living wage to its printers. My very modest salary from the Group School, once I became an official teacher, paid the rent and utilities. We boosted much of our food from the local A&P, stuffing items into the large, deep pockets of our Army surplus trench coats. Dinner for four often consisted of one can of Campbell's cream of mushroom soup added to one can of tuna fish, mixed with a package of egg noodles to make a casserole—filling and, when you're half-starved, delicious.

Denise was very supportive of the Hovey Street Press. She believed the collective was doing important political work by cheaply printing announcements of anti-war demonstrations and posters and pamphlets to promote other Movement work. On at least one occasion, she gave a public reading of her poems as a fundraiser to help with the press' finances. Another time she paid for the printing of a pamphlet denouncing the wide-spread use of anti-personnel cluster grenades by the U.S. Army in Vietnam. When MIT poetry alums Judy Katz and Barry Levine married, Denise arranged for Hovey Street to print a hand-lettered, limited edition chapbook of her poem "A Conversation in Moscow" as her wedding present.

An Unforgettable Dinner

Denise hosted many memorable dinners at Brook Street to celebrate the visits of friends, or her return from foreign travels. There was always a large pot of hearty stew, a dressed salad of greens dusted with freshly cracked black pepper, and crusty, dark, rye bread. Simple but delicious fare. But none of the Brook Street feasts made as lasting an impression as the dinner party to celebrate Denise's return from North Vietnam in November 1972, at the height of the war.

Seated around the dinner table were Denise, Mitch, and their son Nikolai, the two couples who shared their Brook Street house, plus we four members of the Centre Street collective. Before serving dessert, Denise distributed gift items she'd acquired. I recall there were conical, straw peasant hats for the women at the table. Then she passed around several souvenirs she'd brought back from North Vietnam, including an artillery shell.

Richard and I scrutinized the ordnance closely. Alarmed, we asked, "Where did you get this, Denise?" "I picked it up during my visit to an antiaircraft battery outside Haiphong," she replied. It wasn't a spent shell casing the likes of which one could find in an Army Surplus store. This one was capped with its original projectile and had an intact firing pin. Bringing our MIT technical backgrounds to bear, we concluded it posed a threat to life and limb as potentially still-live ammunition. After a lengthy discussion, involving everyone seated at the dinner table, all agreed that it needed to be disposed of immediately. The Charles River was just a 10-minute drive from Brook Street. The BU bridge which spanned it was chosen as the best option.

As I remember it, Richard and I, volunteered to dump the shell, but Denise, who felt responsible for putting us all in danger, insisted on coming along. We drove to the middle of the bridge, pulled over to the curb. Denise got out of the car and tossed the ordnance over the guardrail into the Charles, where it sank out of sight. It beggars my imagination to this day how she slipped the shell through customs upon her return from Vietnam.

It was also at this dinner or during a subsequent visit to Brook Street when Denise proposed that Hovey Street Press reprint a series of colorful silkscreen posters she had acquired in North Vietnam. They depicted peasant women planting rice fields; others riding bicycles weighted down with provision to resupply the army along the Ho Chi Minh Trail. She hoped to auction the reprints to raise funds for Bach Mai hospital back in Hanoi. Three-color lithographic reproduction was a new challenge for the printers at Hovey Street, but one they successfully mastered.

Unlike Denise, Mitch had a hard time finding work, no doubt because of his notoriety from the "Spock Trial." For a time while they were living at Brook Street, he taught several classes at a Tufts University alternative college program established by students and radical teachers there. After that came short-term teaching gigs away at different colleges, punctuated by extended stays at their Maine farmhouse.

Mitch seemed always to be just returning from one of these teaching gigs, or was just about to embark. During this period, I came to think of him as an itinerant scholar/provocateur. He was in the habit of organizing his students, and any faculty he could persuade to join him, in holding teach-ins to raise awareness about the war. Acts of civil disobedience or disruption usually followed.

Denise shared news of Mitch's activities with anyone who happened to be visiting Brook Street, reports which Mitch gave over the phone or in letters. I recall one vivid account of how Mitch had orchestrated a symbolic act of civil disobedience in response to the U.S. mining of Haiphong harbor, blocking the interstate highway that ran through the Midwestern college town where he was then teaching. For this he got fired. No matter what the agreed upon duration of his teaching gigs, Mitch seldom lasted the term. Invariably the collegiate administration found a way to dismiss the provocateur in their midst.

My friendship with Denise grew stronger in the ensuing years as she became my confidante, my poetry mentor, and my guide to a life of the mind broader than just physics and mathematics. I joined her large but intimate circle of friends, social activists, and writers. Coming to study in Boston from blue collar Buffalo, as I did, from a family where books were suspect and my decision to go to MIT instead of a local college surprising, Denise and Mitch offered me the intellectual family and the wider world that I had been searching for.

Where the Highway Ends

In the early 1960s, Denise and Mitch had bought a farmhouse in the township of Temple, Maine—literally where the highway ends. It served them for years as an escape from the summer heat of their Greenwich Village apartment. After they moved to Boston in 1969, when Denise started teaching at MIT, they took off to Temple more frequently as it was closer to the farmhouse. A few years later, in 1973 after they had separated, Mitch took up permanent residence in Temple, while Denise stayed living in the Boston area, an arrangement that was formalized when they later got legally divorced.

My first visit to Temple occurred in the summer of 1972. Denise and I flew together in a small prop plane from Boston to Farmington in western Maine. The twin engines thrummed as we skimmed the green treetops of Maine's endless woods. It was August. Mitch was there to greet and drive us in his Volvo to their Temple farmhouse.

There was always at least one other Volvo parked on the front lawn. Over the years, with each subsequent visit, I would find the collection had grown. Mitch bought them for spare parts to keep one aging Volvo running. His answer to inquiries was always "You can imagine how common a Volvo dealership is in rural Maine."

The kitchen window looked out on a lone apple tree beside a fieldstone fence a short distance behind the house; beyond the fence was a broad, grassy field. It sloped up from the farmhouse to a tree-lined ridge; to the right of the house the field descended sharply in the direction of Temple Stream. A granite slab served as the front doorstep. Denise and I sat there one morning as she read me the poem she'd just written ("In Summer," *The Freeing of the Dust*):

Night lies down
in the field when the moon
leaves. Head in clover
held still.

Mitch split logs, using axe and wedge, sweating profusely in the afternoon sun. In his pedantic fashion, he explained to me the necessity of putting in a winter supply. Mitch was proud of his stack of cordwood.

Mitch delivered endless monologues concerning the leach field. A new—and expensive—septic system was needed, so for a time the outhouse beside the barn replaced visits to the indoor flush toilet. The stack of cordwood formed a corridor you had to pass through on your way to use the outhouse; and, Mitch told me, it served as a windbreak in winter.

One evening Denise ran out the front door shouting, "Time to pick the corn!" Mitch and I left whatever chore we were doing to follow her down the slope to the corn patch. We shucked ears on the run back up to the house, and then plopped them into the pot of already boiling water. The freshest corn I've ever eaten!

Breakfast taken together, consisting of boiled eggs, toast and coffee, was the summer routine at Temple, then each of us retired to our reading or work: Mitch to his novel in the attic loft, Denise to write poems and answer correspondence at her desk in the bedroom. I used the screened-in porch/sitting room off the kitchen as my "study."

After lunch Denise would read aloud the draft of the poem she had been working on. Mitch was always quick to comment on whether he thought the poem a success or not yet finished. Other times she'd share a passage from a letter she had just received from the likes of Bob Creeley, Hayden Carruth, Galway Kinnell, James Laughlin....

On a clear day, standing back of the farmhouse at the top of the sloping field, you could see Mt. Blue in the distance—blue-hued, of course. There were afternoon walks to the top of the field while Denise told me stories about her childhood in Ilford outside London. As she bent to pick wildflowers, she called each by its name: Dutchman's breeches, butter-and-eggs, cowslip, forget-me-not ... names she had first learned from her mother and now shared with me.

Hot summer afternoons after a long, long walk through the woods, we skinny-dipped in Temple Stream. Other afternoons I accompanied Mitch on his errands in the Volvo: to a local dairy farm to buy milk and eggs; to Temple general store to pick up newspapers; to Farmington to buy stationery. Evenings after dinner there was quiet reading in the living room, always punctuated by Denise sharing her enthusiasm for a passage by reading it aloud to her audience of two.

One evening, Denise entertained us with Turgenev's "Bezhin Meadow," from the Hunter's Sketchbook, a reading that conveyed the passionate belief she held that this sketch was a poem in prose. Another evening, Denise looked up from her copy of the Penguin Book of Latin American Verse to make a pronouncement: she really preferred these plain prose translations of Neruda, on facing pages with the original Spanish, to the "poetic" versions done in English by Robert Bly. Then she ran off to fetch her copy of Bly's Neruda, where she showed me she had penciled what she felt were "improvements," which she then demonstrated by reading aloud.

Sometime later, back in Cambridge, following the bloody U.S.-backed military coup that brought Pinochet to power in Chilé, a memorial reading was held in Kresge Auditorium at MIT for Salvador Allende and those who died with him defending his democratically elected government. Denise, among many others, was on the program. She read her "improved" Neruda translations to the overflow audience, while acknowledging Bly's contributions.

Denise led me into the Temple woods on mushroom forays. Among other fungi we found edible boletes and chanterelles. She showed me how she made spore prints of the gilled mushrooms by placing individual caps on slips of notepaper, leaving them overnight, each covered by a teacup. The next morning, we pored over her well-thumbed copy of *Mushrooms of North America*, in the Dover Press edition. Denise admitted, to my astonishment, that unlike both amateur and professional mycologists of my acquaintance, she had never used a dichotomous key for identification, but instead had created her own system of indexing and cross-referencing this tome to aid her in determining genus and species.

At dinner, Mitch always begged off the proffered mushroom appetizers. He hadn't forgotten the time Denise's wrong call of a bolete that turned out to be *satanis* had made her violently sick. Once time, I'd gathered some large parasol mushrooms I'd found growing in the field behind the Temple farmhouse and had fried up for dinner, but try as I might, I couldn't persuade him to sample them.

In later years, whenever I had the use of a car and was planning a visit to Temple, Mitch would ask me to bring him supplies. He was very particular—French roasted coffee, whole beans, not ground, decaffeinated by the water method; and five-pound loaves of his favorite Lithuanian rye bread, which I was instructed to pick up at Spelewski's, a little neighborhood store on Broadway near Kendall Square in Cambridge. The bread was delivered every Thursday from a bakery in Brockton. "Try to get it fresh," Mitch would instruct. "Pick me up at least five loaves. I can freeze them."

In Progress

Mitch had intended to follow *The End of It* with a second novel that he'd started to write in the early '60s, but Vietnam distracted him. He became consumed with anti-war organizing. Then came his conspiracy trial. After that, he devoted all his attention to compiling the big Movement book. Now, more than a decade later, he was trying to pick up the thread of his novel once again but, Denise confided to me, he was having a hard go of it.

In those pre-digital days, Mitch's novel-in-progress took up the entire attic loft in the farmhouse. Each chapter was a neat pile of stacked typescript, with its alternate drafts and notes piled alongside—chapter upon chapter, pile upon pile, spread out on every surface: tables, chairs, and wooden doors laid across sawhorses. Mitch offered to let me read a sample chapter, which I did. It didn't grab me. "It's interesting," I told him. "I look forward to reading more." But he sensed my lack of genuine enthusiasm and never offered again.

Years later, after they had separated, and after he had abandoned the novel, Mitch revealed, in a letter to me from Temple, that when he lived with Denise he had never allowed himself to write poems—she was the poet—but now, he said, he'd realized after their divorce that poetry rather than fiction was his "calling" (Mitch's word). The letter was followed in the mail by a copy of *More Light*, his selected poems published by Mark Melnicove's Dog Ear Press.

Education

On one drive, over winding roads to Temple, Mitch behind the wheel of his Volvo, Denise in the passenger seat expounded on a favorite theme: the young poet starting out—one she later expanded upon in two poems: "The Quality of Genius" and "Growth of a Poet." "You know, Mark," she said, "you're lucky you majored in physics instead of English." Puzzled, I raised my eyebrows. She explained: many young poets she knew had been held back by their formal studies of literature. "It took them years," she said, "to unlearn habits of mind that got in the way of their writing successful poems."

Ever the autodidact, and proud of it, Denise distrusted formal education, which she felt all too frequently resulted in *mis*-education (a word she borrowed from Paul Goodman). Being largely self-taught was a bond she and I shared and often talked about, although our experiences were, at the same time, very different from each other. Until her late teens, she never attended school, but grew up in a household full of books, where everyone read voraciously. "I learned French history," she once told me, "by reading aloud with my mother, all of Dumas and Balzac." In contrast, I was formally schooled, if questionably educated by nuns, but I had grown up in a household virtually without books; and instead of literature I had read for my pleasure physics and mathematics.

Denise liked nothing better than to engage in rapid-fire conversation with other poets and visiting literary scholars, trading insights about her favorite authors—Chekhov, Keats, Rilke, Wordsworth, Shelley, Hopkins.... On these occasions, at both Brook Street and later, Glover Circle, I felt out of my league. I was humbled by the breadth of their knowledge of literature and desperate to "catch up."

59

Poetry

Denise and Mitch both held strong opinions about many things, but especially about literature and politics; they held many of those views in common, but on some topics, they diverged dramatically—and neither was shy to express an opinion, begging to differ if you put forth a contrary one. To join conversation with the two of them together was not unlike navigating the straits between Scylla and Charybdis.

Mitch disagreed with Denise's appraisal of Charles Reznikoff, for one. It was her contention that he never developed as a poet but continued writing the same brief imagistic poems based on observations he made while he walked the streets of Manhattan. Louis Zukofsky, she held, was the more ambitious and hence "greater" Objectivist poet, and gave as evidence his epic poem *A*. Mitch countered, and I agreed, that Reznikoff was the more profound poet. In his view, Reznikoff's pithy poems retained their freshness and grew more resonant with each reading. Unlike Mitch, Denise couldn't appreciate Reznikoff's uniquely American, multi-book epic poem *Testimony*.

Once, just as I was expressing my admiration of Virginia Woolf, whose recently published biography by Quentin Bell was open on my lap, Denise, who never held back her opinions, interrupted: "Don't get me wrong, I love and admire her work," Denise said. "She is an important and gifted writer. But her vision was limited by her social class." Denise added: "How she failed to appreciate Joyce, I could never understand."

Another time, when I was revising poems for publication in my first collection, *The Buffalo Sequence*, Denise admonished me: It was not worth your while, nor was it productive to keep struggling with one poem, trying to get it "right." Sometimes you need to give it up—"abandon" it was the word she used, quoting Valéry. You need to move on and open yourself to new poems.

Still another time, she offered: "Sometimes it's necessary to give up your favorite line or image in the poem you're working on for the sake of the whole." This was after she'd suggested lopping off the last stanza in a draft I had showed her.

Denise always spoke highly of her friend and publisher, James Laughlin; however, using him as an example not to follow, she once warned me against becoming an editor, advice which I clearly did not heed. The occasion was a new volume of Laughlin's poems, which we were discussing, as he had just sent her a signed copy of the limited edition. She said that she considered him a talented poet in his own right, and lamented that he didn't write more poems more often. His use of syllabic verse was a formal choice that Denise said she found both idiosyncratic and interesting—interesting because it sometimes produced "unexpected felicities." Denise thought Laughlin might have developed into an important poet if his own writing hadn't always taken a back seat to his work in the service of those he published under his New Directions imprint, herself included.

Denise professed to greatly value the work of magazine and press editors, admitting that she would find it hard to survive as a writer without their efforts, but she nevertheless thought that becoming one could be the death knell for a poet. Denise believed in the primacy of the poet's calling and jealously guarded her time to write. She often said that a poet needed to keep herself free of commitments to achieve that meditative state that allowed poems to percolate to the surface from subconscious depths. During the height of her activities opposing the Vietnam War, she was very conflicted on this point and often didn't take her own advice.

Although she had mixed feelings about Ezra Pound as both poet and person, Denise was fond of quoting his formulations about poetry. "*Dicten = Condensare,*" was one favorite; and she often referred to Pound's "A Few Don'ts." Pound's formulation of the chief modes of poetic expression—*phanopoeia, melopoeia,* and *logopoeia*—was a shorthand Denise borrowed to characterize the work of any poet she was discussing. I have always thought that Zukovsky's version— the "pleasure poetry affords as sight, sound, and intellection"—was less pretentious, but she favored Pound's Greek.

One of the things that Denise and Mitch agreed about wholeheartedly was that Hayden Carruth's anthology of twentieth-century American verse, *The Voice That Is Great Within Us,* had no rival in terms of the quality of work included and its faithfulness in representing the modernist tradition in American poetry.

Denise held that the vital tradition of American poetry descended from William Carlos Williams, with a seasoning of Wallace Stevens early work. Although she had little interest in the poems Stevens published after *Harmonium*, she adored his prose *Adagia*. "Literature is the better part of life. To this it seems inevitably necessary to add provided life is the better part of literature," wrote Stevens.

Neighbors

The Maine farmhouse was on a graded gravel road that climbed steeply up a hill from the paved Temple Road. Theirs was the second-to-last house. Then the road gave out and became just two ruts.

The farm beyond theirs, where the road ended, had once belonged to Hayden Carruth, although I don't think he ever took up residence there. Mitch and Denise had persuaded him to purchase it with the idea that he would move from Vermont to be near them and to join their growing community of writers. Ted Enslin lived in Temple, as did George Dennison. The Kimbers, Bob and Rita, German translators, lived in the bottomland beside Temple Stream, and Henry Braun and other city writers summered in the area.

Mitch, always keen on making pronouncements, once offered me his appraisal of Carruth's strengths and weakness as a poet. He liked best the poem-portraits Hayden drew of his Vermont farmer neighbors, which were written in open forms. Mitch didn't agree with Hayden that using traditional forms and imposed rules gave greater fluency or force to his writing. On one of my visits to Temple, Mitch spoke effusively about Carruth's latest collection, *Brothers I Loved You All*, newly published by Sheep's Meadow Press. He produced a copy of the book and insisted that I read it immediately.

Denise told me that she and Mitch eventually realized that Hayden was never going to move to Temple. After one heavy snowfall had collapsed the roof of "his" house, they bought him out and gave the property to their son, Nikolai.

Denise found comfort and inspiration in the friendship of people half her age, with whom she surrounded herself, former students and political activists such as myself, whereas Mitch preferred the companionship of his male peers, and was often lonely for lack of it. Lengthy correspondence helped but wasn't an adequate substitute. Denise told me that when Carruth didn't become a neighbor Mitch was far more disappointed than she was.

Years later, shortly before Mitch's death, I read a novella by George Dennison set in Temple (posthumously published by Stearforth Press). I'm convinced that the protagonist—a New York writer transplanted to Maine, divorced, but now with a new wife and children—was largely a portrait of Mitch, or at the very least a composite of George and Mitch.

I once attended a lamb-roast party at Dennison's farm, a Temple summer tradition. Over a blazing fire, a lamb from the Kimbers' flock turned on a spit. There were games and entertainment for both adults and children, and later there was dancing. It was a feast out of Brueghel. All of Temple's urban expatriates were there, plus summer people, writers and intellectuals, with Philadelphia's Henry Braun rounding out the mostly New York gathering.

For a time, Denise had taken German lessons from Bob Kimber. When Denise and Mitch decided to live separately, she took away with her a ten-volume boxed Brecht *Gesammelten Werke*. It was a gift to her from the Kimbers, as Bob and Rita each had one from graduate school and they no longer needed two. She later lent it to me when I began to translate Brecht's anti-war poems (*Deutsche Kriegsfibel*). For a span of five years, as I transported that bulky boxed set while moving from apartment to apartment, I would find scraps of notepaper tucked between pages on which Denise, in her looping scrawl, had recorded her attempts at translation.

Ted Enslin, if I have my facts correct, was already living in Temple when Denise and Mitch bought their farmhouse. I never met him, but from the tales they related of his Maine woodcraft, I formed the image of him as a latter-day Thoreau.

War

In the fall of 1972, just before Nixon's re-election, Denise traveled to Hanoi with fellow poet Muriel Rukeyser and Jane Hart, an anti-war activist and the wife of then Democratic Senator Philip Hart of Michigan. This was obviously a very controversial thing to do; some at the time called it traitorous, as the country was deeply divided over the Vietnam War and the resistance to it. After Denise returned from Hanoi, she and Mitch retreated from the city to spend Christmas in Temple. They invited me to join them. Nikolai was there too. A great snowfall blanketed the fields in soft curves and covered the tree limbs in white. We were snowed in.

I cursed Mitch's ineptitude as I trudged through knee-deep snow in a blizzard carrying an extension ladder up the road to rescue him from where he was stranded on the new roof of Nik's house. He'd climbed up by way of an adjoining shed to shovel off the snow as a precaution but was unable to climb back down by the same route.

An ice storm followed the snowstorm, which left the gravel road slick and impassable for days. Trees and bushes were encased in ice. When clouds finally gave way to sunlight, frozen droplets hung from branches.

Stranded in the farmhouse in remote Temple, we heard news over the radio of Nixon's Christmas bombing of Hanoi. The phone lines mercifully were not down. Denise and Mitch took turns making calls to the outside world—New York, Boston, Washington—trying desperately to mobilize friends, poets, and Movement activists to stage demonstrations against what they viewed as an atrocity. Denise was inconsolable, given to fits of frustration at being unable to vent her outrage. Mitch was calmer, methodical, wearing his organizer's hat.

This was when Denise wrote perhaps her most violent poem, "A Poem at Christmas, 1972, during the Terror-Bombing of North Vietnam," in which she imagined herself an assassin whose targets were Henry Kissinger and Richard Nixon.

The bombing was the precipitating event that led Denise to sever ties with many poets she had long considered colleagues and comrades. The time for reading poems as a form of protest was over she felt, and announced publicly in "Goodbye to Tolerance," another poem written during that winter in Temple. To oppose genocide, she passionately believed, writers, among others, had to, in the parlance of those times, "put their bodies on the line," engage in "direct actions," and "bring the war home." Yet to express her intolerance for tolerance, she had written a poem.

Worried perhaps that I might see an inconsistency in her dealings with fellow poets, Denise offered that she did not hold Hayden Carruth to the same standard of commitment to antiwar activity because he was severely agoraphobic and thus constitutionally incapable of being an activist or even participating in rallies and demonstrations.

Split

One August day in 1973, back in Boston, I sat with Denise on the front steps of the Brook Street house. Mitch was in Temple at the time. Something was amiss; she wasn't her usual perky self. Denise addressed me in a deliberate manner, saying that she had a new poem she wished to read to me, "If that is OK?" Then she proceeded to read aloud "Crosspurposes." (*The Freeing of the Dust*, 1974)

> Two letters passed each other, carried
> north and south.
> In the first was written: "Our journey has come to an end,"

In this way, I first learned of Mitch's decision to pursue a separate life. This should not have come to me as a surprise, but it did nevertheless.

Denise and Mitch were hardly a conventional couple. In New York, they had been members of the emerging avant-garde artist community. As writers and activists in Boston, they each made commitments to read, teach, speak or agitate, which frequently took one of them away from the other for extended periods; in other words, they led lives that were already quite separate. In my youthful naïveté, I romanticized their relationship as "bohemian;" not realizing that, in actuality, they were growing distant from one another. Compounding things was Denise's success as a poet, which in more ways than one overshadowed Mitch's accomplishments.

More telling, in the end, was the fact that, after 25 years of marriage, they were each in love with someone else. It was quickly evident to me that Mitch was having an affair with the young woman he had asked us to put up for a few weeks that summer at our Centre Street collective.

She had followed him east after his recent teaching gig in the Midwest, where she had been his student.

Denise, although she tried hard to disguise and even deny her affections, had been infatuated with Richard since soon after he enrolled in her MIT class. The poems that she wrote over a period of four or five years in which Richard figures attest to this. Richard, however, never fully reciprocated her feelings. He always viewed her as his comrade, his confidante, his mentor, but never as his lover. In keeping with his wish to be "just friends," Denise would try her best to suppress her true feelings, but from time to time she could not stop herself from blurting them out. This always lead to a crisis in their relationship, which Denise patched over by apologizing to Richard for her indiscretion—all things that Mitch could not have failed to notice.

The outcome then, which included their eventual, mutually agreed-upon divorce, was that Denise stayed in the Boston area, moving out of Brook Street into a house she purchased on Glover Circle in Davis Square, Somerville, while Mitch took up permanent residence in Temple.

My friendship with Mitch was strained by their separation, but then was rekindled after his son Matthew (Matty) was born to Mitch and his new wife Sandy. We struck up a correspondence, sharing notes about our experiences as fathers of young boys. I made summer visits to Temple, accompanied by my wife Mary, and son Andrai. Mitch, Sandy, and Matty, would, in turn, visit Boston in February or March each year when "cabin fever" set in and they needed to escape the long Temple winters. Before continuing on to see friends in New York, they would "crash" overnight, or longer, on a mattress on my living room floor or at the Somerville home of my Hanging Loose coeditor, Dick Lourie. (Dick, a student in the very first poetry workshop that Denise taught, had known Mitch since the mid-'60s in New York.)

Musketeers

Denise moved across the Charles River to West Somerville from Brookline Village a decade before the Red Line subway was extended from Harvard Square to Alewife Station, which gradually transformed David Square into the hip entertainment hub it has become today, cheek to jowl now with restaurants and bars crowded with college students and young professionals. But back then, circa 1973, Davis Square was a sleepy Irish, Italian, and French Canadian working-class backwater. Glover Circle was not a circle at all but a cul-de-sac between Meacham Road and Dover Street, one block off the Square. That year, she had begun teaching at Tufts University, just over the Somerville line in Medford, and could walk to the campus.

Denise's house was halfway between two parallel streets, where, after Glover Circle dead-ended, a sidewalk continued, passing by her front gate, completing the passage between Meacham and Dover. An unpretentious rectangular two story wood-frame house, No. 4 Glover Circle was topped with a half-finished attic under a gabled roof; its outside was shingled half burgundy below, half light gray above.

Entering through the front door a long hallway gave way to the kitchen at back; adjacent was a staircase leading up that divided the house down the middle; living and dining rooms were located on the other side. The second floor was similarly divided: Denise's bedroom and a guest room on one side; her study, a single large open room, took up the other side. What had been a sewing room at the head of the stairs, Denise had converted to a library lined with bookshelves. In its cramped quarters, I went to school on her extensive collection of British Penguin paperbacks and New Directions titles, among others.

Denise worked at a massive mahogany desk that stood against the back wall of her study. Its image is preserved in the cover jacket photograph gracing *The Poet in the World*. One window looked out onto the tar-and-gravel roof of the adjacent sprawling one story building, housing a variety of small businesses: a machine shop, a print shop, etc. The view beyond was of the backside of the Somerville theater, which fronted on Davis Square.

The Centre Street collective had dispersed about the time Denise took up residence at Glover Circle. Richard left Hovey Street Press to devote himself to poetry, and rented a studio apartment on Chester Street, just three blocks from Denise's new home. I was sharing an apartment with one of my Group School colleagues in a three-decker on Rindge Avenue, across Mass. Ave. in North Cambridge, a ten-minute walk from Glover Circle.

A magical period ensued, when Richard and I were welcome to stop in at Glover Circle any time. Thanks to proximity, the three of us were all but inseparable. I continued teaching at The Group School, but only three days a week, to allow time for my writing. On my free days, if I dropped in on Denise unannounced in late afternoon, I almost always found Richard already there. Denise, although in other ways a jealous guardian of her creative space, was generous and giving of her time. She afforded us countless opportunities to talk with her at length about poetry, politics, and life in general.

Much in the way that her publisher, James Laughlin, had described Ezra Pound tutoring him in Rapallo at his "Ezuversity," the instruction Denise offered us was informal, taking place across her kitchen table while she opened her mail, over shared meals, or during walks in the park. Other "lessons" took place while picketing or marching in the streets against the Vietnam War as often as when we attended lectures, movies, or poetry readings together.

One night, I accompanied Denise to a rare screening of *The Childhood of Maxim Gorky*, the Soviet film adaptation directed by Mark Donskoy. It was shown at Harvard Epworth Church, one of the numerous venues offering foreign films back then. Denise had seen it in New York many years before, but it was my first viewing. We were both so excited afterward that, immersed in animated conversation, we forgot to catch the bus back to North Cambridge as we had intended. Instead, we walked and talked, talked and walked a mile or more up

Mass. Ave. from Harvard Square, past Porter Square, to Meacham Road where we finally parted company for our respective homes.

Denise was in the habit of opening and sorting her mail each morning at the kitchen table while sipping coffee or nibbling a light lunch in the company of her secretary—Richard and me, too, if we happened also to be there. She made separate piles for bills, for poetry business, for letters from friends, colleagues, and acquaintances, for books and magazines, and for circulars. News of mutual friends or poet correspondents were the first envelopes she opened, often reading aloud to us from their letters. When a copy of a literary magazine arrived that she thought we might find interesting, Denise passed it to us.

Basil Buntings said about one of his mentors, "he put up with [our] presence ... at times when he must have found us intrusive, merely because the young learn from the old and the old must let them." Bunting was writing about W. B. Yeats, but it's a description tailored to fit Denise, too. "Now that I am old myself," Bunting added, "I realize how much kindness was necessary to show such tolerance."

When Denise traveled, whether to Mexico to visit her mother, who had relocated from London to Oaxaca twenty years earlier after Denise's father died, or to England to see childhood friends, or to paying literary gigs—college readings, lectures, or residencies—I'd look after her house in her absence, sharing responsibilities with her secretary. I also performed minor repairs: rewiring a lamp, gluing a rickety chair leg, tinkering with an appliance on the fritz, repainting her basement cement floor, etc.

Those first few years she lived at Glover Circle were lonely, difficult times for Denise, despite the constant presence of Richard and me, and her secretary. Although her separation from Mitch, soon formalized in divorce, saddened her, Denise's poem "A Woman Alone" puts a brave front on that period.

> selfpity dries up, a joy
> untainted by guilt lifts her.
> She has fears, but not about loneliness;

The illnesses associated with her mother Beatrice's advanced age weighed heavily on Denise and caused her guilt for not visiting more often. When her mother wrote from Oaxaca that her spirits were low because her eyesight and hearing, at age 90, were rapidly failing, Denise confessed that her inability to *do* anything about this news frustrated her the most. "I'm the sort of person who needs to do something, to take action," she had said. "I'm not a patient philosopher like my mother."

A few days later, when taking my leave after I had spent the afternoon in her company, Denise walked me to the front door at Glover Circle and, before saying goodbye, leaned her head against the doorframe. "'Unlived life of which one can die,'" she said, quoting Rilke. "My fears for my mother boil down to that. One should be able to experience life up to the last breath." She added, thoughtfully, "the fear of aging is really, I suppose, the terror of losing one's physical capability to experience life. A fear of passing one's last years vegetating in isolation from life. At my mother's age, without sight or hearing, one would have to be an old-style philosopher to endure such an existence."

Denise was also isolated from her poetry colleagues in those years, having broken publicly with many after, derisively calling them "genial" poets, because, although many spoke out against the ongoing war in Vietnam, they lacked her militancy and willingness to condone any means necessary, even violence, to end it. This was a time when she looked to young poets for inspiration, Richard and me, among others. On more than one occasion, she made pronouncements that were digs aimed at her peers: "I find in [young poets'] work a sense of process from which I personally draw more nourishment than from all but a few of my contemporaries, though there are many of those that I <u>admire</u> [emphasis hers]. Curiously, I find more of this same sense of process in the generation of Williams, Stevens, Pound, than in the poets of my own generation. The old masters of the century and the best of the still very young, far though they may be from mastery, share, for me, some peculiar force." (*Hanging Loose* magazine)

Denise was generous to a fault: She realized Richard was in desperate need of a steady income when she visited his Chester Street apartment and saw it was sparsely furnished with items he'd found in the trash, or had crafted from discarded packing crates. It didn't pass her notice that he'd become "skinny as a rail," too. And so she offered to hire him as her secretary. This allowed her to provide him with a modicum of financial support without wounding his pride, while also feeding him.

When I needed dental surgery I couldn't afford because I lacked insurance, Denise fronted me the money, making it clear that she didn't expect me to pay it back. When small press literary start-ups approached her about poets to recommend, she proposed Richard and me, offering to write introductions to our poetry collections, such as the one that graced the Copper Canyon Press edition of my *Buffalo Sequence*. Later, when the books were in print, she brought us along to read in public with her, on a few occasions at paying university events to the surprise and sometimes the consternation of the organizers. And she shared those honoraria with us.

But her generosity extended beyond Richard and me, beyond even other current and former students. Young poets wrote her and sent her samples of their work, unsolicited. She replied to them all and often kept any poems she liked in a drawer for those occasions when little magazine editors asked her to recommend poets they might publish.

She began a correspondence with Jimmy Santiago Baca, who was in prison in New Mexico during those years. He not only sent her his poems but also invited Denise to come west and lead a writing workshop in the prison, which she agreed to do. She promoted his work to editors while he was in prison and afterward. A few years after he was paroled, she persuaded New Directions to publish a collection of his poems for which she wrote an introduction.

At Tufts, she instituted a poetry series for young poets, mostly locals, to provide them an opportunity to gain experience reading their work in public and helping them to gain some visibility. Richard and I each read in this series, as did Judy Katz-Levine, Steve Blevins, and Tino Villanueva, among others.

She had a modest budget from Tufts to bring published authors from out of town to read and visit her classes. She often put them up in her guest room at Glover Circle and hosted dinner parties for them to which I was always invited. Among the poets I met on those occasions were Robert Mezey, David Bromige, Keith Wilson, the Iranian dissident poet Reza Baraheni, and Afro-American poet and painter T. J. Reddy.

Reddy, a civil rights and anti-draft activist in North Carolina was framed in 1972 for setting fire to a stable that killed more than a dozen horses. He was labeled a political terrorist and given a 20-year sentence. When it came to light that the witnesses who helped convict him were paid by the government to give false testimony, he filed one appeal after another, even reaching the Supreme Court, but all were denied. Denise, among many others, wrote letters in support. Then in, 1979, he was pardoned by the governor of North Carolina. The author of two poetry collections, one written before, the other during his incarceration, *Less Than a Score, But a Point* (Random House) and *Poems in One-Part Harmony* (Carolina Wren), Denise arranged for him to read at Tufts after he was paroled. She put him up at Glover Circle and hosted a gathering there to promote and sell his paintings. Steve Blevins, her secretary at the time, and I helped arrange the paintings for display in the living and dining rooms and entry hallway of Denise's house. She favored Reddy's Chagall-inspired oils with Afro-Caribbean images and bought two.

Tribe and Tradition

To have gathered from the air a live tradition
or from a fine old eye the unconquered flame.
—Ezra Pound, Canto LXXXI

Denise saw herself as belonging to a poetic tradition that extended back through Pound and H.D. to Yeats, Swinburne and even further back to the Romantics: Keats, Shelley, Coleridge and Wordsworth. On this side of the Atlantic, she affiliated with poets who took William Carlos Williams as their master, a modernist tradition that continued forward through the "Objectivists," on to Charles Olsen and the constellation we know of as The New American Poetry that included, among others, Robert Duncan, Robert Creeley, and Denise herself. This was a tribe I aspired to join.

But she never thought of herself as entirely an American poet, and not a British one either; rather she felt she was a poet whose heritage was as much continental European as anything else. In a letter to William Carlos ("Doc") Williams (circa 1960), she once wrote, "Certainly, I am an American poet, if anything—I know I am not an English one—nevertheless I feel the great European poets 'belong to me' as an inheritance, too." And so, as one of her protégés, my exposure to literature was broad, deep, and international in scope.

Before accepting the faculty position at Tufts, Denise had very much been an itinerant poet/teacher, which required her to travel to colleges and universities around the country for a few weeks, a month, or a semester at a time. Whenever she traveled abroad, accepting speaking engagements in Europe, or visiting childhood friends in England, or her mother in Oaxaca, she sent postcards. One card she sent me from Europe depicted Brunnenburg Castle, built in the 13th century, overlooking Merano in the Italian Tyrol. "Dear Mark," her message on the back read, "I'm staying in this very castle—have marked my window. Mary de Rachewiltz, E. P.'s daughter, & her family live here. It is incredibly beautiful, within & without." In her characteristically unconventional fashion, Denise had taken ballpoint pen to the picture and circled the window of the castle room that she occupied.

E. P. was, of course, Ezra Pound. His daughter, Mary, was Denise's friend and Italian translator. This was the same castle where Yeats had once been a guest and where Pound took up residence after his release from St. Elizabeth's Hospital. Denise told me on another occasion that while visiting there, she had written letters and composed poems, making use of the antique Remington that some of the *Cantos* had been typed on. There she had sat in Yeats' chair and had lived amid Pound's personal collection of Gaudier-Brzeska's sculptures and drawings.

Robert Creeley, in an interview I once read, likened the experience of an apprentice, learning by imitation from his master, to plowing a field. Learning to plough, he said "is both watching someone else do it and then taking the handle of the plough and seeing if you can imitate, literally, his way of doing it, therefore gaining the use of it for yourself." In Denise, I had the good fortune to watch a master as she went about her work, and then to try out for my own purposes the "tricks" and "tools" she had employed, while still under her watchful eye.

That kind of intimate guidance gave me the palpable sense of being inducted into a guild, whose secrets are passed down, master to apprentice, from one generation to the next—and certainly I was aware enough of modern literary history at the time to understand something about what that consisted of, although I was not yet confident enough in myself as poet, or in my calling, to believe I was a deserving acolyte. But I quickly learned that once you were admitted to Denise's anointed circle, she took a keen interest in everything you did that became resources for your poetry, and that she followed your progress with rapt attention as you explored your own ways of working, slavish imitation being the farthest thing from her mind.

One Pilgrim's Progress

Denise viewed her own life in art as a pilgrimage, a seeking out and following of uncharted paths, some of which turned out to be dead ends, which then required her to double back and set out in another direction. One day when I stopped in at Glover Circle, she prefaced my day's "lesson" by reading me a quote she had just come across by the Russian critic Victor Sklovsky: "A crooked road, a road in which the foot feels acutely the stones beneath it, a road that turns back on itself—this is the road of art."

She thought about the growth and development of young poets the same way. Provided you had the stamina, provided you persisted in striving to find your way, she believed that you would continue to reach new and higher plateaus of achievement, which, if you didn't always recognize them right away for yourself, she was always on hand, ready to point them out to you. This, literally, was language she used in discussing new poems I would show her. "With these poems," she would say, "your work has reached a new plateau."

She had a keen sense of timing about when to offer encouragement of just the needed kind. One such instance occurred during my first year after college when I was living and teaching in Santa Barbara and questioning my poet's vocation. I'd sent her a compilation of all the new poems I'd written since our MIT workshop had disbanded. She responded with a ten-page letter from Oaxaca, where she was visiting her mother. "You have grown so much in your poetry," she wrote. "I'm really thrilled at your development. ... of all the people in the [MIT] class you've gone the farthest (and you started at almost zero).... you're really doing good stuff." I was, of course, buoyed by her response and reenergized in my writing, even though I very much doubted that I had "gone the farthest."

In those early days, I frequently despaired that I was mostly stumbling in darkness, but Denise would invariably step forth at the right moment and illuminate my way, reminding me that, "Our doubt is our passion. And our passion is our task," quoting Henry James. "The rest is the madness of art."

False starts and mistaken directions, however, were things Denise did not hesitate to point out as when I wrote a long poem of over 200 lines about a teenage boy from a Cambridge housing project, whose beating death at the hands of the police lead to several days of rioting in the streets of East Cambridge. She took a keen interest in my first-hand reports of skirmishes between the police and housing project denizens and how teachers like myself, social workers, community organizers and other social activists got swept up in those events. She encouraged my involvement, but when I showed her the ballad that I'd written which romanticized this street urchin victim as a modern-day Robin Hood, she didn't mince words. She called it a "sociological" poem with cardboard-thin characters, lacking the complexity and individuation of real people. Such a frank appraisal was not easy for me to take, but in this instance, I came to realize that she was right.

But when I showed her new poems she thought were a breakthrough in my development as a writer, she used the phrase "coming into a new country." To my mind, filled with 1950s TV pablum, this phrase conjured Fess Parker in the Disney film version of *Daniel Boone*, crossing the Alleghenies via the Cumberland Gap into Kentucky— "new" territory despite its native inhabitants!—but I suspect the image in Denise's mind was something out of Bunyan's *Pilgrim's Progress*.

The day I read her the first several poems of what would become *The Buffalo Sequence*, was such an occasion. She literally leapt up from her chair to hug me, exclaiming, "That's it! That's it! You've found your voice!" After that epiphany, I could only stumble down the steps of her house and onto the sidewalk, transported by the knowledge that I was "on the right path" and had not "lost my way" in this uncertain and unmapped enterprise.

My ABC of Reading

Denise shared with me anything she was reading that excited and inspired her. I did likewise. Whatever her newest enthusiasm, I went right out and read it, too—and sometimes vice versa. Often, I was discovering for myself writers whose work Denise had gone to school on long before; but, occasionally, my excitement after reading one made her go back and consider the work again, reappraising and deepening her appreciation of that writer, or so she told me. The great Portuguese modernist Pessoa was an example. I was amazed to discover the poetry he'd written under a variety of heteronyms, each distinctly different in style and subject matter. Denise admired his poetry, too, and thought his talents were unique.

Denise was passionate about the great 19th- and early 20th-century masters of Russian literature: in prose, Turgenev, Dostoyevsky, Tolstoy, and her beloved Chekhov; among the poets, Pushkin, Blok, Akhmatova, Pasternak and Tsvetaeva. She, in turn, caught the infectious enthusiasm I had for the work of early Soviet writers: Mayakovsky, Yesenin, Babel, and Paustovsky, among others.

But we didn't always concur. When our opinions were at odds about some author or body of work, she would hear me out, parse the precise points of disagreement and then patiently explain to me, without being pedantic or condescending, why she held firm to her view. She usually chalked it up to differences of taste, but there were a few occasions when she felt that I was just dead wrong and told me so.

Gorky was the one author whose place among the pantheon of great Russian writers we disagreed about. I valued some of his socialist realist prose a lot more than she did. But what we *did* agree about, with regards to the "father of Soviet literature," was his autobiography. We

81

were both smitten by it, especially the first volume, *My Childhood*. We also both adored *Reminiscences*, Gorky's memoir about Chekhov and Tolstoy at Yasnaya Polyana, Tolstoy's country retreat, a place Denise had once visited. Not one but two well-thumbed copies of *Reminiscences* sit on my bookshelf today, but those two copies give me a pang of guilt. I had originally borrowed the book from Denise's personal library. After devouring its contents, I just had to own a copy for myself. It was then out of print, but I scoured used bookstores in Cambridge and Boston, and eventually found a copy of the exact same edition. Afterward, with my own copy in hand, I must have neglected to return hers.

I suffer no such guilt over my copy of Kropotkin's *Memoirs of a Revolutionist*. That volume had been the personal possession of Denise's mother Beatrice, who shared with Denise a devotion to the ideas of the "anarchist prince." Denise presented it to me as a memento after her mother's death because, near the end of her life, I had befriended Beatrice in Oaxaca. The original inscription, in Denise's hand read "Love from Den & Mitch," and beneath it, in her mother's hand "(For June 29th, 1971 my 86th Birthday)."

This fervid indoctrination to Russian literature points to one of the most important things I learned by observing Denise at close hand; namely, how as a poet to read widely and deeply, assimilating influences without becoming imitative. She had the ability to absorb lessons from the writers she admired in what I can only describe in alimentary terms. She would often respond to my inquiry about what she had learned from writer X or Y by saying, "I'm still chewing on it," or, "I haven't entirely digested it yet." Eventually, the fully assimilated insights she took from each one mixed with others in, what Henry James called, "the well of unconscious cerebration" and later emerged as something wholly her own.

The poetry of Cesar Pavese is an example of this. She read a selection of his poems from *Lavorare Stanka*, translated by William Arrowsmith that appeared in the *American Poetry Review* sometime around 1975. Her enthusiasm for these poems put her on a quest to find more. She turned up a Penguin prose rendering of the poems, which she said she preferred. Pavese's poems appealed to her at a time when, as she states in a preface, she was disenchanted with the overly ego-centered, confessional poetry being written by many of her contemporaries.

Pavese wrote as an observer about the lives of common people, peasants, workers, etc., noting their actions, dress and demeanor, and imagining their stories, their inner lives. Always an acute observer herself, someone inclined to create imagined narratives for strangers who caught her eye, Denise was inspired by Pavese's way of working in the *Lavorare Stanka* poems, and so turned her gaze outward at a time when she was often quite depressed and guilt-ridden about the dissolution of her marriage and about her aged mother's rapidly declining health. The result, a sequence of poems titled, "Homage to Pavese," was unmistakably written in her own voice, but spoke in a new, quite different mode or manner. My favorite was about the *serape* seller who plied his trade in the Oaxaca *zocalo*:

> Decades he has passed
> back and forth and around and back and forth
> in this square; and always the weight
> of many *serapes*, heavy, and in the sun, hot,
> on his shoulder.

A Life of the Mind

Most importantly, during the years when I was starting out, Denise, by her own example, gave me the confidence to believe that to develop as a poet I did not need to be enrolled in a graduate writing program. (Back in the early 1970s, MFA programs had not yet proliferated to anywhere near the degree today.) Rather, it was only necessary that I "continue to read and write, and to be open to whatever might befall me;" as had been her own pathway, "the rest must depend on my native abilities and the degree of intensity and persistence that I was prepared to devote to the service of the art." This was something that she had gotten from her deep immersion in Rilke's life, letters, and poetry.

I sometimes wondered whether, despite her passionate engagement with living friends and acquaintances, the realm of literature and dead writers wasn't in some way more real to Denise than flesh and blood people. She was on "intimate" terms with Keats, Chekhov and Rilke. She adored these writers more than any others. I can think of no other way to describe her passionate embrace of mind and heart. She spoke of them in my presence as if they were still living friends and colleagues, ones that she conversed with daily. In "Memories of John Keats," an early poem dedicated to her husband Mitch, Denise had written, "*Watchfulness and sensation* as John Keats / said to me / for it was to me / he said it / (and to you)." Although she meant it figuratively, a part of her believed Keats spoke literally to her, too.

Keats, Chekhov and Rilke were such vital presences in her life that their words and ideas populated her conversation and thinking. Keats: "I am certain of nothing but the holiness of the heart's affections, and the truth of imagination." Chekhov: "Faith is an aptitude of the spirit. It is, in fact, a talent: you must be born with it." Rilke: "Be patient toward all that is unsolved in your heart and try to love the questions themselves."

Once, at a poetry reading—"You remember, Mark, you were there."—she was asked during the Q & A, whether she memorized poems; were there certain poems that she knew by heart? "I personally have never been able to memorize anything other than a few nursery rhymes," was her reply; adding that she struggled unsuccessfully to commit the multiplication tables to memory. The exception, she said, was when, as a child, she had memorized Keats'"Ode to a Nightingale," over a period of months because she decided that if she should ever be wrecked on a desert island—as her child-self hoped she might be—she would need to know some poetry by heart, "even though," she said, "'Ode' wasn't a poem very suited to a desert island."

Observing Denise's relationships with the likes of Keats, Chekhov, and Rilke and seeing how they informed her life and her poetry was a revelation to me, one that gave me permission to discover my own pantheon of writers and over time to become intimate in my own way with their words and thoughts.

Denise taught me, first and foremost—and this is another lesson she passed down from Rilke—to *experience* what you live: to the artist, whatever is *felt through* is not without value, for it becomes part of the ground from which you grow." Lastly, by being in her presence during those years, I acquired a deep appreciation for what the vocation of art really means: that"obstinate devotion to which," as she wrote in an essay ("Rilke as Mentor") "though it may not lead to any ordinary happiness, is nevertheless at the opposite pole to the morbid self-absorption often mistakenly supposed to be typical of artists."

Principles and Opinions

"Those are my principles, and if you don't like them ... well, I have others."
—Groucho Marx

"You know that I believe one shouldn't tailor one's writing to the working-class or the poor," Denise said to me one day. She wasn't asking a question but rather making a statement. We were discussing William Morris as model political activist/artist. The role of the politically engaged poet had been a topic of our conversations going back several years: the poet as witness, the poet as chronicler of struggles for equality and social justice, the poet as voice of the people, the poet as radical visionary, etc. The focus of these discussions had been the poets and writers one or the other of us was reading at the time, ranging from South Americans Pablo Neruda and Cesar Vallejo to Central Americans Ernesto Cardenal and Roque Dalton to continental Europeans Bertolt Brecht and Vladimir Mayakovsky ... and now the Englishman, William Morris.

When I knew her, Denise's ideas about poets and poetry, her principles and her opinions were already fully formed. She held them firmly, and seldom if ever, in my experience, modified them. Unlike Groucho Marx, she took them seriously, and had little sense of humor about them. "It is not the responsibility of the individual writer to increase the literacy of the masses," she went on to assert that day. "To assume oneself responsible and able to do so would be arrogant. A complete upheaval of the social order is necessary to achieve that. It is rather the individual writer's responsibility to work toward a revolution. A working person with little education but who is turned on to reading can comprehend the most complicated poem. Those people, poor or working class, for the most part uneducated or poorly educated—mis-educated—who aren't turned on to reading … the individual writer can't be held responsible for the fact that they can't be reached."

Denise took a keen interest in the growth and development of young poets. During the time Richard and I were daily presences in her life at Glover Circle, we served as case studies for at least two poems she wrote: "Growth of a Poet" and "The Quality of Genius." Her high regard for us, however, once led to our embarrassment when we would have much preferred that she'd kept her opinions to our intimate circle. The occasion was a benefit poetry reading for Medical Aid to Indochina to a packed hall in the Charles Street Meeting House. After Richard and I read our own poems, it was Denise's turn. She began with "The Quality of Genius", telling the audience afterword that, although not mentioned by name in the poem, she considered the two of us geniuses. Mortified, I turned to see Richard's response. He just rolled his eyes back into his head. I knew he felt, like me, this was just plainly inappropriate in that setting, however flattering her intention.

On our drive back to Glover Circle that night after the event, Denise riding in the back seat of Richard's car, we made repeated attempts without success to persuade her that that public forum was no place to reveal private opinions shared among friends. But she adamantly held her ground. "When it comes to my firmly held convictions," Denise insisted, "I do not make distinctions about where or when or to whom it is appropriate to express them."

I had many close friends and activist comrades in the audience that night. For a long time afterward, they took great pleasure in pointing out every stupid or thoughtless thing I said or did, followed by the teasing, "Nice going, genius."

One of Denise's principled stands resulted in losing me a friendship. After the Centre Street collective dispersed, some of us regrouped in a house in East Somerville. I invited Denise to dinner to meet the members of the reconstituted collective. When she arrived early, I took her into the living room. There, I introduced her to one of my new housemates, a feminist lesbian who was a bit star-struck. But things went badly, quickly. Eager to impress Denise, this young woman enthusiastically described her day job as an Evelyn Wood Speed Reading instructor.

Denise just sat back in her chair and repeated the words "speed reading" several times; then, leaning forward said in no uncertain terms that she was diametrically opposed to anything associated with reading for speed.

Invoking the pleasure principle, Denise launched into a lecture: "Reading," she said, "should be a slow, sensual enjoyment of how words make meaning, including an appreciation for the syntax, texture, and sonority of their arrangement." My new housemate offered a feeble defense, but then went silent. I was stunned by Denise's insensitivity, but I didn't know how to salvage the situation. My housemate never forgave me, believing I had set her up to be attacked. To no avail, I tried to explain that Denise held strong opinions and was undeterred about sharing them regardless the company or occasion.

Denise believed, on principle, that any poetry written with a particular audience in mind, was, more likely than not, inferior, suffering from self-imposed limits. She gave as one example the poetry written for children, most of which, she believed, was not poetry at all—just verse. "It's not fully poetry," she argued, "because it talks down to children both in vocabulary and in subject matter." And, she noted, "wise children, of which there are many, don't like it very much because they can tell that it's not poetry." She added, "They may not be able to define what poetry is but they *are* capable of recognizing it when they do read it."

Denise's "tryout" for a faculty position at Tufts University came when she substituted for poet and English professor X. J. Kennedy during his sabbatical year. I always wondered whether she had ever shared these views with Joe Kennedy, who was an acclaimed practitioner of verses written for children. Knowing that her principled integrity always trumped propriety, I couldn't imagine Denise holding back her opinion if the subject ever did come up between them. A genial man, Kennedy's own poetry sat squarely within the camp of traditional poetry for which Denise had little sympathy. That said, I never heard her utter a disparaging word about his person or poetry, or ever single out his children's verse for criticism.

Preferences

One of Denise's stubbornly held opinions out of touch with the times (early 1970s) had to do with gay men, of whom she knew many as acquaintances, as colleagues, and even as close friends. She held that their sexual orientation boiled down to an arrested adolescence, fostered by overbearing mothers. I gave up on trying to persuade her this was simplistic. It drove Ron Schreiber crazy. Ron had known Denise since the early '60s in New York, when as a Columbia graduate student he had enlisted her as contribution editor to *Things* magazine, the precursor of *Hanging Loose*. An educator, poet, and my dear friend and Cambridge neighbor, Ron was a prominent gay-liberation activist, a member of Boston's Good Gay Poets collective, and one of the first college professors to create and teach a gay and lesbian literature course. I observed him lock horns with Denise on this topic at several dinner parties; more often, he expressed his exasperation to me privately.

Denise ignored or failed to notice that her opinion about gay men in the abstract were contradicted by her relationships with two of her dearest friends and former students, both of them gay male poets. Aaron Shurin had studied with her in Berkeley and afterward followed her East to Boston. Later, when he returned to the West Coast, they kept up an intimate correspondence (see her poem "Writing to Aaron," *Life in the Forest*, ND). Steve Blevins, the other, also her student, had followed her East from Cincinnati and served as her secretary at Glover Circle four or five years in the 1970s, a time when I was a frequent visitor to her home/office. When Steve later contracted AIDS and eventually died from its complications, Denise arranged in his memory for a posthumous collection of his poems to be printed with an introduction she wrote.

Before, and then after Steve served as her secretary, Denise hired a succession of women to file, type, and assist with her business correspondence and travel plans, usually former students, and frequently lesbians. Her relationships with each of them was at odds with her equally controversial and untimely opinions about their sexual orientation. Suzy Groden, an Amherst College classical studies graduate, served as Denise's secretary when she first settled in Boston. Denise spoke admiringly of Suzy's translations of Sappho. I'm certain she couldn't have missed noticing that Suzy's lovers were women. Nevertheless, Suzy was one of Denise's long-cherished friends and remained so after her employment as secretary ended.

Denise first knew Linda Falstein as a Chicago anti-draft activist and partner of draft resister Dennis Reardon. Later, when Linda resettled in Boston, she and Denise became close friends and remained devoted to one another, bonding over more than just their political activism, even after Linda came out as a lesbian.

Denise viewed her long-time friend Muriel Rukeyser, if not exactly a mentor, as a kind of "big sister;" ten years older, she was the age of Denise's actual sister Olga. Muriel served Denise as a role model, bridging political activism with poetry. Their friendship dated from New York in the early 1960s when, together, they participated in Ban the Bomb protests and civil rights demonstrations. At the height of the Vietnam War, they traveled together to Hanoi, and together they later campaigned for the release from prison of the South Korean dissident poet Kim Chi Hah. I always assumed Denise knew that Muriel was a lesbian, as anyone reading her poems had to realize—I certainly did; plus, Denise was acquainted with Muriel's longtime partner Monica McCall. And yet, years later, while sitting for an interview, Denise expressed genuine surprise bordering on distress, after her interrogator mentioned Muriel's sexual preference for women.

Denise died more than a decade before same-sex marriage laws were enacted, so I can only speculate, but I feel certain she would have, in this regard, remained consistent in her contradictions: congratulating her gay and lesbian friends and embracing their unions despite her discomfort with their sexual orientation.

Women's Poetry

Another subject about which Denise took issue was "Women's Poetry." In the early 1970s, the Women's Movement engaged the daily lives and conversations of everyone I knew; women, of course, but men, too, if you were involved with liberated women. "Women's liberation" was taken as seriously as opposition to the draft and ending the Vietnam War. Denise herself was certainly in many ways a "liberated" woman. She took lovers at will, pursued a career as a prominent poet without gender inhibitions in a male-dominated literary world, and became a public figure in her outspoken opposition to the Vietnam War and in her anti-nuke activism. "I didn't suppose my gender an obstacle to anything I really wanted to do," she wrote. But when the topic turned to Women's Poetry she would have none of it. Yes, she was a woman, she asserted, but not a woman poet, a category she felt limiting; she was, she insisted, just a poet, period!

Denise professed both publicly and in private, that she never felt discriminated against as a writer; never felt her inclusion in anthologies celebrating new trends in poetry were token gestures, whether appearing alone or with only one or two other women: e.g., Kenneth Rexroth's *The New British Poets* (1949) and Donald Allen's *The New American Poetry* (1960). "That genre may be determined by gender [is] an idea I find extremely foreign to my own experience," she wrote. Another time she said, "I never made an aesthetic decision based upon my gender." As a young poet starting to publish in the US, she was lionized by such prominent elders as Rexroth and William Carlos Williams, among other males, but although humbled by their admiration, she felt she deserved their accolades.

The first time I heard Denise take a public stand against Women's Poetry was a talk she gave at the Harvard Divinity School in 1973, where I was in the audience. Her topic was "trends in contemporary poetry." The proliferation of anthologies of poetry by women, she began was, in her view, a negative trend. She said it troubled her to admit this because she did feel solidarity with the Women's Movement in general, but she found these anthologies full of unsatisfying poems, a lot of it not art but rather self-expression. (Woodberry Poetry Room recording) Ironically—and another example of her inconsistency— at about this same time, she compiled an anthology of young women poets for *Trellis*, a small magazine based in West Virginia.

The argument she elaborated against Women's Poetry came down to this: although art does contain the self-expressive, its underlying impulse is to make objects of words, or whatever medium the artist is working in, objects that will be able to stand alone after the maker has moved away and no longer needs these products for the self-expressive purpose that impelled their creation. But too much of the women's poetry she felt failed this test; it remained self-expression at its core.

The women I knew at the time all belonged to women's consciousness-raising groups. Their participation helped them gain self-confidence and find strength when confronted with a male-dominated world. They viewed women's writing groups and women's poetry anthologies as extensions of that kind of solidarity. When I made this argument to Denise, she expressed sympathy with these mostly younger women, but discounted the last links in their chain of reasoning. Group solidarity, she countered, failed them when it came to their poetry. Denise believed poems written with the aim of telling the world what the position of women really is, or poems written *by* women *for* women inhibited the inner freedom to let the poem have its own exploratory life. A poem must lead the poet into new realizations, she believed, and not merely allow the poet to state what she or he knew beforehand. When that freedom is violated, Denise contended, the result is bad poetry.

Denise sometimes came across as preternaturally contrary. At the same Divinity School talk, James McIntyre, who was also on the program spoke first; his topic "Poetry and Piety." He concluded his remarks by saying that we Americans, are dreadful to our poets:

Pound in a cage, etc. Denise immediately distanced herself from McIntyre's remarks when it was her turn to speak, stating that she disagreed that society treats poets poorly. "I'm out of sympathy with too much sympathy for artists," was her memorable way of putting it. The mythology of the "hard lot of the poet," she went on to say, when spread by poets themselves is self-indulgent; when spread by others sentimental. "It is easier to be a poet than many other things," she said, "One is very lucky to have the ability to write poetry. The harder lot falls to those many who have not, or who have not found the capacity to utter or speak out of themselves."

Those remarks paralleled her critique of Confessional poetry and the idolization of contemporary poet/suicides such as Sylvia Plath, John Barrymore, and W. D. Snodgrass, etc. (Robert Lowell's suicide occurred a few years later). When Anne Sexton committed suicide in 1974, Denise published an essay in the Boston *Real Paper* articulating her stance ("Anne Sexton: Light Up the Cave"). This was boldly controversial. Sexton was much loved and admired in the Boston literary community and beyond; but in this instance, I thought Denise was right on by attacking the prevailing association of poetry with self-destruction. In her essay, she countered Sexton's example by citing instead life-affirming ones, artists such as Hokusai and Thoreau.

III. JOURNEYMAN

"The Ezuversity was an ideal institution for a twentieth-century goliard.... The classes usually met at the lunch table. They might begin with Ezra [Pound] going through the day's mail, commenting on the subjects that it raised."

— James Laughlin, *Pound As Wuz*

Glover Circle Notebooks

My poetry "career" was already launched, largely through Denise's agency, when I first began to record our conversations in my notebook. *The Buffalo Sequence*, my first poetry collection, was slated for publication by Copper Canyon Press, with an introduction by Denise. My future even held the prospect I might be able to support my baby son and his mother on my salary as poet-in-residence for the Worcester, Massachusetts, public schools, a job Denise had recommended me for. My apprenticeship was completed, and I was starting out as a journeyman poet; but I knew that I still had much more to learn from her.

In the years preceding, I had absorbed, sponge-like, every utterance that issued from her about life, literature, and politics. The knowledge I acquired fed my growth and development as a poet. But now, teaching children and coaching their teachers, I felt the need to articulate my ideas about poetry. In an effort to put down on paper what I had learned from Denise, I began keeping the journal from which the selections that follow are taken.

Another impetus for making this record was nostalgia for a more carefree time in my life, now past, when I could just drop in on Denise anytime I knew she was at home. But commuting by bus and train fifty miles each way to Worcester, three days a week, combined with childcare responsibilities, meant my visits to Denise were curtailed and required advanced planning. Had I taken for granted the ready access I had previously had to her? It seemed more precious to me than ever now that the occasions to talk to her about poetry and listen to her expound were fewer and farther between. This gave added urgency to my efforts at recording our subsequent talks and my reflections upon them. Although there are entries about Denise both in my earlier and in later notebooks, they are fewer, briefer, and far between, nothing as sustained as the period covered here, which lasted until the complexities of my life made it impossible to sustain.

From Glover Circle Notebooks

Spring 1975
The other day, I came across my copy of *A Conversation in Moscow*, the limited-edition chapbook of the poem Denise had enlisted Hovey Street Press to print as a wedding gift for Barry and Judy. Rereading it, I had this thought: my long-held contention was not quite right that anyone who had never enjoyed the experience of engaging Denise in face-to-face conversation could gain a reliable sense of the richness and of her talk by reading this poem. Evocative though it is, missing is the visual dimension; namely, the ways in which Denise's hands punctuate and illustrate what she is saying.

Denise enjoys friendly argument and uses her hands expressively to emphasize each point she makes. Her gestures can be taken for a barometer of the intensity of her engagement with the topic under discussion. One night recently, I observed her among a group of people, sipping wine and talking, Denise at the very center of the animated conversation. The fingers of her two hands were laced together, clasped tightly, as if in prayer, which she shook in an agitated fashion. She seemed impatient, restraining herself out of politeness from interrupting the person speaking, while she perched at the very edge of her seat, ready to pounce at the first opportunity to interject the urgent thought on the tip of her tongue.

Undated 1975
Denise described to me with a sense of appreciative awe the practice of the French pediatrician LeBoyer, who she had just read about in a magazine article. "He places the infant in a bath of warm water immediately after birth; then he turns his head and looks away as he

holds the infant there, cradled in his hands. He says the reason he turns away is 'not to intrude upon the newborn's privacy during those first precious moments of its life in this world.' Imagine!" Denise exclaimed.

Undated 1975
Giving Denise a lift to Tufts today, I introduced her to Carol S., who was in the passenger seat, a neighbor and friend to whom I was also giving a lift. Carol is a nutritionist who works in East Boston, I explained to Denise; and I told Carol that Denise had lived in Eastie when I first met her. Denise piped up from the back seat, "Do you know X? She was once a student in my writing workshop." Carol did know her. Denise then qualified her comment, "Well, actually, she was not a student-student. It seems I always allow at least one non-official student into my writing classes—sort of like 'adding leaven to the lump.'"

Undated 1975
Denise mentioned today that she had gone to a bassoon concert the other night with Stevie [Steve Blevins, her secretary]. She repeated the word bassoon, emphasizing and stretching out the second syllable, "basS-O-O-O-N," her lips puckered as if sipping soup from a spoon. "It was a concert given by a basS-O-O-O-N quartet," she added, unable to resist savoring the word once again.

March 29, 1975
Denise and I were talking in her living room today about David Bromige, who had just returned to Berkeley, where he lives and teaches. She had arranged for him to read his poems at Tufts and had put him up at Glover Circle during his visit to Boston. She had encouraged Richard and me to attend his reading, but I wasn't able. "He used to write good poems back when I knew him in Berkeley," she told me, but then quickly followed with a disclaimer, saying that she had not been inclined to like the poems he has been writing lately since he had fallen under the influence of Creeley and the Bolinas scene.

At Richard's Passover Seder a few days ago I had ample opportunity to speak with and observe Bromige, but took a dislike to him, finding him to be cynical, arrogant, and egotistical. I could tell that Richard had a similar reaction, which did not go unnoticed by Denise.

"It's too bad you didn't meet David under better circumstances," Denise said today. "There is a whole other side to him you would have liked. He and I spent the next day [after the Seder] together, chatting, and had a wonderful time. There are certain things we were able to talk about that I am unable to share with either you or Richard."

I didn't press her to explain what she meant. I just assumed she was referring to the fact that she and Bromige shared a common British heritage. They were both born in London. Ten years her junior, he was much closer to being her contemporary than either Richard or me. She is, after all, the age of our mothers. Also, Americanized though she is, having married Mitch, raising a son in New York, and immersing herself in the American poetry, I nevertheless feel at times that there is a cultural gulf between us. This has everything to do with her British middle-class, almost Victorian upbringing. Another factor is that she never had to suffer through the oppressive boredom of public schooling, but instead was home-schooled and grew up in a highly literate household where reading and book knowledge were prized.

After a long silence during which I sensed that Denise was savoring the memory of her conversations with the now departed Bromige, she repeated, "You know, Marek, there are many things I can't talk to even you or Richard about. It is a painful separation I feel between us. Although there is ever so much that we *do* share, my talks with David satisfied something I had been missing."

September 8, 1975

I hadn't seen Denise for two months until today; hadn't written to her, except to send a card from San Francisco; hadn't received any letters from her during that time either. This summer, Jan and I drove cross-country with baby Andrai. We spent a month in San Francisco as guests of Jan's friend, Cathy Walkup, publisher of Five Trees Press. I babysat Andrai during the days, while Jan, already an experienced offset printer, learned to hand-set type and then print using Cathy's platen press. Before our departure, Denise had given Jan as a project a manuscript of ten poems written by her mother, Beatrice, to set in type and print as a limited edition sheaf. Denise intended to surprise her mother with her own first poetry publication!

Denise filled me in today on her own summer activities. She told me that she had been to Oaxaca to visit her mother, who had just turned 90. She returned with Richard's [Edelman's] mother-in-law, Angelina. Denise said that she had spent many evenings with Richard, Olivia, Angelina and their friends in Somerville, until Angelina returned home to Mexico City.

Denise also told me she has been meeting with her twenty-five student advisees at Tufts this past week. Classes will start tomorrow for her. Denise is relaxed and buoyant in conversation, showing no evidence of the strain she felt last spring.

"I am amazed at how young these college freshmen are," Denise said. "It is strange, particularly when one thinks of how grown-up high school seniors seem to be. It's as if they regress the summer between graduating from high school and entering college."

As a teacher," she continued, "one is always struck by how much and how quickly the students you had as sophomores, say, seem to have matured over the summer months, when you meet them in your classes as juniors. It happens each year: freshman to sophomore, sophomore to junior … I've noticed. You must have seen much the same with your high school students. But what is it that mysteriously happens the summer between high school and college that so adult seeming high school seniors are transformed into mawkish college freshman?" she asked.

"One of my students, a girl, stands out from the rest like a sore thumb," Denise continued. "You can tell by her accent, she is from a working-class family. The rest are from middle-class and upper-middle-class families; there is even one Roosevelt from Oyster Bay. I have never before experienced a college registration," Denise revealed. "It was total and absolute confusion. This girl, more than any of the other students who came to talk over their schedules with me, was disturbed by it. She wasn't sure whether or not she should continue in Latin or take instead a French or German class." Denise mimicked the student's girlish voice: "'She had had two years of Latin in high school and had done well at it. Perhaps she *should* continue in Latin. But then, maybe she should branch out and try a different language, which might be of more practical use to her. But, of course, she did well in Latin....' she ran on like that" Denise continued. "I sensed that she would feel more secure taking Latin and so said to her, 'Yes perhaps you should take Latin seeing as you had done so well at it.' Later, when she had returned from talking with the Latin instructor who is, at the same time, I believe, the entire Latin Department, she said, 'Oh, he was such a nice man. He said that it didn't matter how much Latin I knew; it only matters that I wanted to study and learn. Oh, he was such a nice man!'" Denise chuckled, "I think she had fallen in love."

Undated, Fall 1975

"Reading my poems to college audiences, I find, more and more often, I am confronted by uncomprehending stares," Denise blurted out today, completely out of the context of the conversation we were having. "More and more, I find myself giving long introductions to the poems I am about to read, explaining what certain lines allude to—and not personal or obscure literary references by any means. College audiences strike me, each year, as being less and less literate. Don't college students read anymore?" she asked, as if expecting me to know the answer because I had been a college student myself not that long ago. "It has gotten to the point," she went on before I could even respond, "where I felt it necessary to footnote certain poems in my most recent book [*The Freeing of the Dust*]—allusions which five years ago, I would have expected my readers to know."

September 9, 1975

"I have started a new sequence of poems," Denise told me today. "It will be titled 'Homage to Pavese' [later published in *Life in the Forest*, ND 1978], inspired by a collection of his poems in translation that I have been reading. He is much better known for his prose. There's little of his poetry in translation." I knew a little about Pavese from reading several of his poems printed in a recent *APR* [*American Poetry Review*] in English versions by William Arrowsmith. They were a selection from his forthcoming translation of the complete *Lavorare Stanca* (*Hard Labor*). But Denise was referring to a British Penguin edition in her possession translated by Margaret Crosland.

"I was inspired by how Pavese writes about other people instead of writing about himself always," Denise went on. "He does of course write about himself, but somehow his writing has the quality of presenting himself as one among many, rather than being overly ego-centered as are so many contemporary American poets."

"There are only four poems in this sequence so far," she told me as she handed over the manila envelope containing the typed copies. "There is the poem about my mother ["The 90th Year"] which you saw before; the poem to Aaron ["Writing to Aaron," addressed to Aaron Shurin]. I showed you that poem, didn't I? A poem titled "Woman Alone;" and a poem I wrote this summer while visiting my mother in Oaxaca, about a serape seller. I was always intrigued by that man, shouldering his heavy load of serapes from early morning until very late into the night, even wandering about the *Zócalo* when everything, or nearly everything is closed-up and there are no longer any tourists about to spread open his serapes. There is a poem in my latest collection (*The Freeing of the Dust*, ND 1974) which is sort of a precedent for these poems, particularly the one about the serape hawker, but it doesn't have the same depth or detailed imagining into the life of another as the serape hawker poem has."

"These poems are, I feel, a reaction to the intensely personal poems I had been writing this past spring, in particular, that batch of love poems I wrote ["Modulations for Solo Voice"]. I am comfortable now, with my position as a 'woman alone'. I enjoy being able to sleep late if I wish to on Sundays when I am not teaching; not having to prepare dinner at a certain hour; or like this not eating dinner at all but for a little salad late in the evening."

At this point, we were interrupted by the telephone ringing in her dining room. Denise returned to the kitchen after fifteen minutes on the phone and explained: "That was your countryman, Jerzy Kosinski." We both laughed at the word 'countryman.' This was a private joke between us referring to my renewed identification with my Polish heritage and insistence on the Polish pronunciation of my surname, Pav-lak, instead of the Americanized Paw-lack.

"He and I will be reading the same weekend at a conference for English teachers, in Falmouth, Mass. I was curious for more information about him and his writing, since I've always been somewhat suspicious of him."

"Suspicious?" I asked. "I know that censorship is pretty stiff in Poland," was Denise's reply, "but nowhere near so bad as in the Soviet Union. I wouldn't deny anyone leaving the country if they are given an opportunity; but as long as there is some chance to change things, to challenge the authority of the bureaucracy, I feel one should stay and fight. I mean ... all right, things are pretty bad, and one may have to leap at any opportunity to leave that comes one's way, but why come here? Why come to killer America? I can't believe that people behind the Iron Curtain are all that naive, or that the censorship is so great that writers don't understand what America symbolizes. Why can't they go to Sweden? Anywhere but here!"

September 20, 1975
I'm a notoriously bad speller. This is compounded by the fact that I'm also a poor, hunt-and-peck typist. Despite consulting the dictionary and correcting every noticeable (to me) typo, the typescripts of my poetry manuscripts still contain errors. Today Denise didn't have her usual pencil in hand as she read the new poems I shared with her. I watched nervously as her eyes went down the page, shaking her head as if to shoo away a bothersome fly every few lines. When she could no longer withhold her irritation, she looked up from the typescript and after a thoughtful pause said, "You know, I used to worry about your poor spelling, because it is common that a person who can't spell either does not or cannot hear the sounds of words properly. That would be fatal for a poet. But yours is a different problem, I think: carelessness. Reading your poems over the years has convinced me that you *do* hear the words properly, but misspell them anyway." I was crestfallen. I had gone over and over these poems. I really had tried make them perfect before I dared to show them to her.

Denise is all for copyedited manuscripts, but has discouraged me from revising poems over and over. She has at times scolded me that doing so is a waste of time better spent on writing new poems, unless, of course the rewrite is a true re-*vision* of the original. I showed her some poems recently that I had re-visioned, to which she gave her nod of approval.

After a long pause, she then said: "It is difficult to make a selection from the body of yours and Richard's writing that will accurately demonstrate what each of you are attempting to do. In Richard's case, it's because his poems are so long and Gongoresque in structure, that selecting passages from them does not do justice to the whole. In your case, it's because you are really writing out of an aesthetic, which someone reading your essay on the Oral Tradition would realize. Individual poems by themselves don't show all of what you are doing with language. That's why it is important, I feel, for the body of your work to appear in book form. The same goes for Richard."

Undated Fall 1975

It is not unusual for me to find Denise preoccupied and lost in thought when I drop in on her. If she happens to be mulling over a topic that we have talked about, she'll freely share her latest thoughts on the subject. Sometimes she will run upstairs and return with a quotation bearing on the subject that she had copied out on a slip of paper and pinned to the wall in her study. Other times, she'll read to me from her notebook ... a quotation she copied out, or a reflection on something she recently read, or her latest rumination on one of her "habitual preoccupations" about the nature of poetry and the work of the imagination. Occasionally these "ruminations" have resulted in poems. When they do, she is always eager to share the newly minted work with me. A few days ago, she retrieved from her study the manila folder containing her latest work and read to me "The Growth of a Poet;" on another occasion, "The Poem Rising by Its Own Weight." The growth and development of young poets, such as Richard and myself, as well as others of her students both past and present, has been at the forefront of her thoughts lately.

At other times, Denise will be occupied by daily chores, removing the dishes from last night's dinner from the dishwasher, for example, or asking my advice about adding insulation to her attic, when something said in the course of our conversation triggers a switch. Then, it's as if she has withdrawn from the room to some other place or plane. She becomes lost in thought. The light in her eyes is like that of the moon in the depths of night, peering down through clouds. It is on such occasions that I imagine she is engaged in some inner dialogue or argument with the great writers of the past, Rilke, or Chekhov ... similar to what I read about Ahkmatova, who was said to have carried on an inner dialogue with Pushkin about an argument he had made about poetry and the Russian soul a century before.

October 8, 1975

Steve [Blevins, Denise's secretary] and I were talking at her kitchen table when Denise entered through the front door this late afternoon, looking tense and exhausted after her long day of teaching. For the next hour, she didn't stop scurrying from room to room, looking, all the while very businesslike dressed in a pants suit, the jacket of which she never took off. Up the stairs, down the stairs; opening and reading mail; looking quickly through the pile of books and magazines that had arrived today; making phone calls, now from the downstairs living room phone, now from the phone upstairs in her study—whichever was nearest when the thought struck her; writing out notes for correspondence that Steve would later answer; sending him on errands to fetch things ... and all the time, knitting her brow as if trying to remember what it was she had told herself she must remember to do when she got home from school today.

Passing the living room chair in which I sat reading, trying to stay out of her way, Denise stopped and turned, looking as if she only then realized that I was in present, and she addressed me: "I had the opportunity today to read the student evaluations of my last term's class. Their only criticism was that they had found it to be more disorganized than the class which preceded it. By 'disorganized,' I feel they really meant the material in this second semester didn't hold their interest the same way the poetry in the first term had. I had covered in the second term poets who might not normally be treated in an undergraduate poetry course— 'good' poets such as Keith Wilson and Bessmillar Brigham, as you know. This illustrates for me the difference between 'good' poets and truly 'first rate' poets, such as Williams, Galway Kinnell, or David Ignatow."

Undated, Fall 1975

Denise told me that a few days ago, "that truly Indian Summer day," as evening was coming on, she went to close her front door left open the afternoon for the breeze, and noticed her neighbors' three-year-old son, Levin, standing alone outside on their front porch, which faces her own front porch. "He was not actually standing," she corrected herself, "but leaning, his chin propped on his palm, his elbow resting on the porch railing. He was gazing wide-eyed after people passing on the sidewalk between our two houses, headed toward Dover Street."

"I watched Levin a long time without his noticing, but didn't call out to say 'Hello,'" Denise went on, "for fear that he might become self-conscious. How wonderful to see so young a child not needing adults to entertain him, but secure and taking obvious pleasure in being alone —luxuriating, really, in being left to himself with only his imagination to entertain him!"

October 21, 1975

I attended a conference of New England Teachers of English in Falmouth, Mass., this weekend. Denise was the guest speaker/reader at the luncheon. I was invited, along with four of my colleagues from the Massachusetts Poets-in-the-Schools Program, to read my poems later in the day as part of a "poets' coffeehouse." I had arrived late to the conference, missed the morning program and most of the luncheon, but just in time to catch Denise reading to a crowded room.

About halfway through her program, Denise announced that the title of the next poem she would read was "Letter to Marek About a Photograph." I tried unsuccessfully to catch her eye before she started, hoping to send her a non-verbal message, "Please, don't call me a genius, or say some other thing that will embarrass me." I know from experience that Denise sometimes doesn't observe discretion and will publicly share her opinions about people and things that are really private matters. She told the audience that Marek was Polish for Mark, and that the poem was dedicated to Mark Pawlak. So far so good, I thought, but then she added, "He is one of the poets who will be reading later in the day." I could feel my face flush. I silently prayed she would finish and hurry on to the next poem.

I felt conflicted. On the one hand, I was honored that she had dedicated this poem to me. (She had given me a copy a few weeks ago.) How many other young poets can claim to have a friend and mentor such as Denise? She has done everything in her power to encourage and support my work and aspirations. She has fed my growth and development as an artist with books, conversation, perceptive insights and friendly criticism. That poem is an example of her "infeeling comprehension" and a testament to the depth of our friendship. But, all that is just between the two of us. On the other hand, I have wanted my poems to be taken on their own merits. I felt that by identifying me as one of the poets on the program later in the day, she had singled me out among my peers as someone she had anointed and in so doing; although well-meaning, she had overstepped a boundary.

October 31, 1975

I asked Denise why it is that I have never seen one of her books reviewed in the Sunday *New York Times Book Review.* "About ten years ago," she explained, "they used to regularly ask me to write reviews. I did it for a while but found such reviewing to be the making of catty remarks about other authors, and that became distasteful to me. I eventually made a pact with myself not to do so any longer and began to turn down the offers from the *Times,* until they realized what was up and they stopped asking me. I think the editors were offended that I would turn them down because they never once since have run a review of any of my books, which they always used to do."

* * *

111

I told Denise that at a recent poetry reading by Robert Bly, which I attended in Worcester, he lectured the audience about Yeats's style of oral reading, and demonstrated how Yeats would accentuate the vowel sounds in his lines. Bly went on to claim, I continued, that Yeats was the first one since the Beowulf poet to discover and make use of the vowel sounds in English. However, a few days after I had heard Bly say this, I happened to be reading Ford Maddox Ford's reminiscences of his childhood in which he describes just this a style of reading as a 'fad' among dilettante poets in drawing rooms of the 1880s, all of whom were imitating Tennyson. "Yes, yes," Denise said. "There is a recording in the Lamont Library at Harvard of Tennyson reading aloud. I happened to have heard it played over the radio the other day. You can distinctly hear him drawing out the vowel sounds." Denise went on: "But of course it was Yeats who wrote about that style of reading, and if you listen to recordings of Pound reading his own poetry, you will notice that his style of reading is in a direct line from Tennyson by way of Yeats. I respect Bly's love for poetry, which I feel is genuine and sincere," Denise added, "But most everything he claims to have—quote—discovered—unquote—Robert Duncan knew twenty-five years before him."

* * *

Denise often drops tidbits about her childhood when I'm in her company, such as this one today. When I arrived, I had found Denise in the kitchen talking to the young woman who does her housecleaning. The woman was lamenting the fact that she hadn't won this week's lottery. This prompted Denise to tell the story of how as a young child she had picked a British derby winner. "I used to listen to the radio quite a lot. One time I happened to catch the broadcast of one of the big horse races and picked to myself the name of the winner. The horse I picked had a seafaring name. I wanted as a child to be a sailor for some reason, although living in the suburbs of London I'd never seen a sailor. In any case, my horse was not one of the two or three favored to win the race, but it won anyway. You can imagine how surprised I was. So there was a short while that I would everyday look in the newspaper at the racing listings and pick a horse whose name struck my fancy, and invariably it won—childhood intuition! So you see, for a time, I was a sort of 'rocking-horse winner,' but mind you, one unexploited by adults; neither of my parents being very worldly: my father a scholar and a clergyman, and my mother ... well, a virtual innocent."

November 12, 1975

I stopped by Glover Circle to return to Denise her copy of *Discretions* by Mary de Rachewiltz [a memoir, largely about her father, Ezra Pound], which I had borrowed. It was dusk. There were no lights visible in her house as I entered the alley, so I assumed no one was at home. I thought to enter by way of the back door and leave the book on the kitchen table for her to find. But it turned out that Denise was at home, in the kitchen preparing dinner, so that I startled her when I opened the door with my key. I apologized for bursting in, explaining that since she is usually still at Tufts at this hour, and not seeing any lights on, I had assumed she was not yet home.

After her initial surprise passed, Denise told me that she had stayed home all day, ill with a cold and sore throat. She elaborated, saying that she had simply lounged about the whole day listening to music while correcting student papers. "In fact," she added, bending from the waist and making a grand, swooping gesture with her hand and arm, theatrically pointing to her pants legs, "I had just this moment changed from my lounging clothes into these slacks. I had thought that I would go out and keep an engagement I'd made weeks ago, but I now think that I'm still not well enough and ought to stay in."

Denise asked me what I thought of the book I had laid on the table. I told her that my previous impression of Pound as a cold, gruff man was somewhat tempered by his daughter's portrait of him. "Yes," Denise remarked, "considering that they [Pound and her mother, Olga Rudge] weren't going to bring Mary up themselves, they probably did the next best thing by shipping her off to a Tyrolean foster family." She added, "But then when she was older, they shouldn't have been so ruthless in taking her from the only security she had known at Gais."

Denise, unprompted, continued talking about her friendship with Mary de Rachewiltz—cooled of late—and what news she had of her through their mutual friend Jay Laughlin. All the while that she was talking, Denise moved back and forth in the kitchen removing plates and pots from the stove top and placing them in the sink to be washed. I remained standing at the kitchen table, knowing that if I sat down I would stay too long to run the other errands I had yet to do this evening.

"It's a tragedy for Mary, as it would be for any writer, that she has virtually no 'mother tongue' other than the Tyrolean dialect" Denise told me. "The cultural uprooting she continually underwent at her parents' whims left her without one. Her English is always a bit off, as is her Italian. And although her friends have suggested that she make Tyrolean her literary language, I doubt that she will."

Denise paused midway in her rounds between stove and sink whenever she needed to search within herself for the right phrase, sometimes gesturing vaguely in the air as if to give shape to her impressions of her friend. At one point, vigorously wiping stains from the stove top with a piece of crumpled paper towel she added, "That she has something of a Puritan spirit to her is the only explanation I can give for the way she idolizes her father—her virtual worship of his image and her dedication to translating the *Cantos* into Italian." Noticing some stains on the linoleum floor, Denise stooped and now even more vigorously began rubbing them out as she continued to speak. "She refuses to think of pursuing her own writing until she has finished translating the *Cantos* in their entirety, which I have argued with her to no avail is foolish. But she will at the same time complain that she never gets down to her own work, to satisfying her own creative needs."

At one point, Denise mentioned that Mary de Rachewiltz lived in Cambridge. This came as a surprise to me. I had always thought that she lived in her castle [literally] in the Italian Tyrol. I had this impression from a postcard Denise had sent me during one of her European summer trips a few years ago, when she had visited Mary there. The postcard showed the castle perched on a mountainside. I found nothing in reading *Discretions* that would have led me to think otherwise. Compounding this misconception on my part was an occasion when I had met Mary's son, the young Baron de Rachewiltz.

This occurred when he was passing through Boston and was the dinner guest at Denise's Brook Street commune in Brookline. He had talked that evening about his collection of tools used by the Tyrolean peasants and of his plans to open a museum of these farm implements in one wing of the castle as soon as he returned home.

Another misconception of mine that this same conversation dispelled was that Denise and "Pound's daughter," as I had thought of her, were, if not intimate friends, then at least on very good terms. I knew that Mary was the Italian translator of Denise's poems and I felt certain that she had spoken of her with affection on other occasions. The coldness with which Denise now described Mary de Rachewiltz's hang-ups about her father and her inability to get down to her own work surprised me. But perhaps I shouldn't have been, given that I have often heard Denise express impatience with any talk about "writer's block."

I have heard her speak derisively when someone has mentioned their fear of never writing another poem, or never finishing another book. This seems to be something Denise herself has never experienced, something she has little sympathy for in others. Whenever Denise has gone without writing poems for any stretch of time, rather than complain of "writer's block" or express anxiety about writing new poems, she has instead spoken positively about such fallow periods as times when she is assimilating new influences, ideas, and experiences—the stuff of future poems. She has as much as said that the creative unconscious has a natural rhythm of its own that cannot be rushed. Because one is not putting pen to paper, she has explained to me, does not mean that there is inactivity in the unseen depths of ones being, activity that might eventually surface as poems.

November 25, 1975
Nik is in town visiting [Nikolai Goodman, Denise's son, a year my junior, who was then living in NYC]. My arrival at Glover Circle had interrupted their discussion of Carlos Castaneda's *Don Juan*, which Nik has been reading. He took up where he had left off when I arrived, explaining Don Juan's philosophy to Denise: ordinary reality, according

115

to Don Juan, is merely illusion. "Like the Hindu concept of Maya," Denise offered, "the phantasmagoria or illusionary dream of duality in the phenomenal world?" "Yes, that's right," Nik, responded. "But then how is it," Denise asked, "that this man who lives in harmony with his surroundings, with the flora and fauna, and who sees our world, our reality as illusory, how is it that he speaks of himself as a warrior? I would have thought," Denise continued, "that someone who is in harmony with his environment would be compassionate or at the very least non-aggressive." Nik patiently explained that Don Juan's self-image as "warrior" is a defensive stance against the people he lives among who see only the illusory world of "reality"; being a warrior is his response to them. He is not passionately engaged in his "warrior's" persona; rather he is a disinterested warrior.

Something about this conversation struck a sympathetic note in Denise. Her eyes lit with excitement as she raised both her hands above her head and exclaimed, "Oh!" Then, after a moment's pause, she began to rummage in her book bag, which sat beside her on the kitchen floor. "Let me show you something I read to my freshmen class today," she said. "It has a very similar idea in it ... from Yeats's well-known poem, 'The Fisherman.' Imagine an Irish peasant fishing in a stream by some boulders ... and the poet says

> ... Before I am old
> I shall have written him one
> Poem maybe as cold
> And passionate as the dawn.

"'Cold and passionate,'" Denise went on. "We normally associate passion with heat; if not always hot, then at least warm. But Yeats is accurate in his observation that the dawn is cold and that it is also associated with passion ... the color of light at dawn. Cold passion has embodied in it that idea of standing back from the illusory world. It is a theme common in Yeats's work,"

Rummaging in her book bag again, Denise pulled out her well-worn cloth-covered copy of Yeats's *Essays and Introductions*. "Let me read you something from an essay Yeats wrote titled, 'The Moods':

> ... argument, theory, erudition, observation, are merely what Blake
> called 'little devils who fight for themselves', illusions of our visible
> passing life, who must be made serve the moods, or we have no part in
> eternity. Everything that can be seen, touched, measured, explained,
> understood, argued over, is to the imaginative artist nothing more
> than a means, for he belongs to the invisible life, and delivers its ever
> and ancient revelations.

After reading this passage, Denise laid the book upon the table, her right hand resting on the open page. She looked past me out the window, lost in thought. Then, turning her attention back to Nik and me, she stated buoyantly, "You know, I really sounded forth to my freshman class today. I think I astonished them. There was a dull, glazed look in their eyes when I had finished. Perhaps in doing so I didn't allow for any response. No one said a thing. It wasn't, however, a full class because of the holidays, and most of the brighter students were absent, the ones who I rely upon to read as a barometer of whether I'm reaching the class."

Denise stopped speaking, having caught herself sounding condescending. She laughed; then added self-deprecatingly, "I sound as if I had dropped pearls of wisdom in the mud." Then, correcting herself, she added, laughing again and imitating the tone of an intellectual snob "No. No. I sound as if I had dropped pearls of wisdom into a pen of intellectual swine." At this we all three rocked with laughter.

When our laughter had subsided, Denise again picked up the book of essays and thumbed through its pages looking for something, saying as she did so, "I read my class a passage from another Yeats essay today called 'The Symbolism of Poetry.' Here it is ... let's see, he wrote it in 1900, so that would be five years after the first passage I read. It explains why in contrast, 'The Moods' is a much less mature statement of the same thing:"

> All sounds, all colours, all forms, either because of their preordained
> energies or because of long association evoke indefinable and

yet precise emotions, or, as I prefer to think, call down among us certain disembodied powers, whose footsteps over our hearts we call emotions; and when sound, and colour, and form are in a musical relation, a beautiful relation to one another, they become, as it were, one sound, one colour, one form, and evoke an emotion that is made out of their distinct evocations and yet is one emotion. The relation exists between all portions of every work of art, whether it be an epic or a song, and the more perfect it is, and the more various and numerous the elements that have flowed into its perfection, the more powerful will be the emotion, the power, the god it calls among us.

When she had finished reading this selection, we all sat silent savoring the way Yeats articulated these beautifully wrought ideas. Then Denise opened her volume of Yeats's *Collected Poems* and read aloud "The Fisherman" poem again, this time in its entirety.

November 25, 1975

Nik: thick, straight, black hair; bushy black eyebrows; high cheekbones; square jaw.... Although I've known him for years, I still can't get over how the most striking features of each of his parents are combined in him. He and Denise had finished dinner and were sitting at the kitchen table, talking about her mother, his grandmother, when I arrived and interrupted them. "It's like when you're a kid and you hurt yourself," Nik was saying. "The pain is never as bad as you had imagined it would be. It's not so hard to take; it hurts less than a sympathetic onlooker would imagine."

Denise invited me to sit with them. She poured me a glass of wine. Nik continued, arguing that Denise imagines a more difficult and frightening existence for her mother, than she, Beatrice, actually experiences. [Denise's mother, Beatrice Levertoff neé Spooner Jones, has lived in Oaxaca, Mexico, for almost two decades as the adopted *abuela* to a Mexican family. I spent several afternoons visiting with her there the summer before, while traveling throughout Mexico]. According to reports from Denise, her mother's physical health has deteriorated significantly since I saw her. At 90 years of age, she is going blind and deaf. Denise has told me that she is seldom able to go out of the *hacienda* on her own now. She agonizes over her mother's condition, the more so because of the geographic distance that separates them, and for the fact that she depends on infrequent letters for news of how her mother is feeling.

Nik went on to say that the things one must to do out of necessity to carry on with one's life, place certain limits upon how much pain the sufferer can allow herself to experience and keep on with living. After a point, he said, the sufferer simply must marshal her faculties and draw on reserves of strength and simply carry on. Whereas, he argued, for the person looking on from a distance—meaning Denise—there are no such limits to restrain her imagination of the pain her mother is suffering. "Grandma may be weary of living, but she still has a lot of fight in her," Nik said. "She can still summon the strength to go on with the day-to-day demands of her life."

Nik's presence has a calming effect on Denise, who has lately been tense, nervous, argumentative, and anguished about her mother since she last visited Oaxaca and saw for herself her mother's state of decline. She listens attentive to all Nik says, rarely interrupting him. She trusts his perceptions and is almost happy and comforted by his presence.

November 25, 1975

The exiled Iranian poet Reza Baraheni is Denise's dinner guest. He read earlier in the day at Tufts. His poems document the horrors of the Shah's regime, under which he was imprisoned and tortured. He has a new collection of poems translated into English, and so he is touring the U.S. to draw attention to the plight of intellectuals living in Iran under the Shah. He's a very good poet and a man of sharp intellect, not to mention courageous.

Richard was unable to attend his reading and this dinner. After I have shared some of my poems, Denise read several of Richard's poems for Reza to appreciate. He was curious to know which poets Richard and I read that influenced us. Denise interrupted by characterizing our education in poetry, Richard's and mine, with a reference to Balzac's novel *The Black Sheep*. She ran upstairs to retrieve her copy of the novel and read a passage she had earmarked: "that deep and serious education which can only be had from within oneself, and to which all talented men have devoted themselves between twenty and thirty years of age."

I was able to speak for myself, but because Richard was absent, Denise described Richard's habits: "His interests are narrow," she explained," his reading has many gaps but is characterized by a single-minded intensity. He devours everything in the path of his focus." As she spoke, she raised her cupped hands to her temples to suggest a horse with blinders.

December 9, 1975

I was "guest poet" at Denise's Tufts writing workshop today. Several of her students had told her that they liked my poem from *The Buffalo Sequence* that Denise had tacked to her office wall, so she thought to invite me to read poems to the whole class. After doing my part and answering their questions, I stayed for the remainder of the class.

At one point Denise addressed the group: "I should think that a young American poet could get a complete and fully rounded education in poetry by reading no other twentieth-century poets than William Carlos Williams and Wallace Stevens—so wonderfully complementary they are. Stevens, delicate, sensual, with a tendency toward verbosity, is able to touch his subject so lightly, so subtly. And Williams ... spare, energetic, not that he isn't sensual, too, but his touch is never soft like Stevens; he tends rather to be more earthy."

Two students read aloud poems they had written in response to an exercise in syllabics that Denise had given them in a previous class. In the discussion that followed, Denise talked about the advantages and disadvantages of artificial structures when writing poetry. This led her to the subject of rhyme. "One must be careful if one is to use rhyme," she warned, "not to be lured into saying, for the sake of it, what one had not intended to say; that is, being seduced into placing words in the poem solely for the sake of the patterned rhyme that have no relation to what you feel and perceive.

"On the other hand, rhyme used properly and effectively has the advantage of leading the poet to images and/or symbols perfectly suited to the poem; sometimes to real discoveries he would not otherwise have come upon. I'm thinking specifically of the greatest poet to write rhymed poetry in English in the twentieth century, William Butler Yeats, though he did have his roots firmly planted in the nineteenth century.

"So unobtrusive is his use of rhyme," continued Denise, "that, often, it is only after rereading one of his poems that one is aware there were rhymes present at all. He was unique, I think, in that he was seldom, if ever, led to say what he hadn't meant to say by the need for a rhyme. His poems are like the clothes sewn by a master tailor: the pockets and zippers are so carefully disguised that one doesn't at first notice there are any at all. It looks at first glance to be a seamless garment."

December 9, 1975 (an additional note)
I met Denise at her office to walk with her to her class, but since I arrived early and she had things to attend to I sat in a chair in a corner of her office and perused her bookshelves. I gathered from notices posted in the corridors and the conversations I had overheard between students and the English department secretary that it must be registration period for spring semester at Tufts.

There was a knock at the door. A student peeked in to ask if he might have a word with Denise. She invited him in, scrutinizing him intensely for a few moments, trying to place him, until the spark of recognition lit up her face, just as he was about to explain who he was and what he was inquiring about. "Oh yes," Denise said, turning to her desk and shuffling the papers on it "I have your poems right here." She held up a sheaf of pages stapled together and waved them about.

Her expression grew serious as she searched for the right words. "Before I say that you are admitted to my poetry workshop, I want to know why you want to enroll in this class in particular, and what you hope to get out of it. You see," she explained, "there are many people I shall have to turn away since I have to limit the size to fifteen, and I want to be certain that I have selected a compatible group."

Denise waved the student's poems about as she spoke, unconsciously dangling before his face the admissions ticket he so desired. Denise was quite unaware that she was making him nervous. He stammered, but

121

Denise spoke before he could utter a word of explanation as to why he might be considered a suitable addition to her class. What was most important to her when selecting students, she explained, was that each exhibit a willingness to learn from the others, for ostensibly that was the environment she sought to foster and not one in which the students looked only to her as the source of all knowledge.

She saw her role, she went on, as a facilitator, one who, because she had more experience in reading and talking about the qualities of poems, could jump-start the class discussion, but that once gotten going, would step back and allow the students to talk to one another. It was her job, she said, to make sure that the conversations about students' poems were sincere and constructive, and conducted in a spirit of mutual regard and helpfulness.

She added, still dangling the sheaf of poems before his face, that she was looking for a median level of writing experience in the students she admitted to her class because this insured a common ground for sharing work and knowledge about writing. Although, she admitted there will always be a range in any class of skill, talent, and experience as writers, she had found that individuals who were well on their way to being poets often did not benefit from being in such a class and ended up dissatisfied. "If you feel yourself to be a competitive person; if that is the atmosphere you need or find stimulates you to do your best work; then my class is not for you," she continued, "and I would have to ask you to dis-enroll."

The student took his poems back from Denise, thanked her for explaining her criteria for admission to her class and turned and left— fled down the corridor really—without getting a definitive answer as to whether he had been let in.

I felt sympathy for this student. It was only six years ago that I had stood in his place, presenting myself and my juvenile poems to Denise, seeking to gain admission to her poetry writing class at MIT. I remember feeling tongue-tied in her presence and unable to offer but a few words in explanation about why I wanted to join her workshop, about what I had to offer, and what I hoped to get out of it. The experience had, literally, given me a nightmare at the time.

December 14, 1975

Denise came to dinner to see our new apartment. Afterward I drove her home. During the car ride, I asked whether, in addition to her creative writing workshop, she would be teaching a large lecture course on literature again in the spring semester. I expressed my concern that the work of preparing such a class and grading student papers without the aid of a TA had severely taxed her energies this fall. No, she told me, she would not be repeating that course. Although she still wouldn't have a TA's help in the spring, the class she was slated to teach was limited to only fifteen students. It shouldn't be that much work, she added, since it was the kind of course she liked teaching, one in which she planned to match poems written by a variety of poets with their statements about poetics. "We will read such things as Lorca's *Duende* essay," she told me knowing that it was one of my favorites. Denise added, "I'm at my best as a teacher when I can think out loud and my audience finds it interesting." The aftertaste of her first disappointing performance as a teacher lingered in her voice.

Last week she had received her student evaluations from the lecture course she had taught. There had not been one good word in any of them. "Surely," she had said aloud, as much to herself as to me that day in her office, where I was visiting, pushing the pile of evaluations across her desk in my direction, "surely, I couldn't have misread all those expressions I took to be excitement and interest?" As we neared her house, Denise added this final note on the topic: "I am best before an audience of students who are self-motivated and present because they are interested in what I have to say. Ones who don't need to be told what to do, but can think for themselves."

Undated Fall 1975

"... No! No! The poem is about *actual* wood doves," Denise corrects, "actual wood doves in the woods of Temple, Maine." She is sitting at one end of her living room couch facing another woman at the opposite end, who had misunderstood her poem "Knowing the Way" [from *Footprints*] as *only* metaphorical, and not about real wood doves seen, observed. Denise is being interviewed; there is a cassette tape recorder between them. The woman is French, but speaks English fluently with a noticeable British accent.

"Of course, the poem *is* metaphorical on one level," Denise continues. "The dove being a symbol of peace. I wrote it at a time during the anti-war movement when I felt that aggressive action had to replace passive resistance as a strategy. Against our common association of the dove's soft cooing utterance with passivity, I wanted to contrast the swift, bold flight of the wood dove of my actual experience. A poem *can* have *only* literal meaning and still be a poem. I think of such poems as 'plain' poems. But, myself, I prefer that layering of meaning upon meaning which metaphor allows. However, any metaphor deserving the name must in poetry arise from the literal; and the layering of one meaning upon another must never obscure the literal reading of the poem."

How quick Denise is to leap upon misconceptions about poetry or on attempts to mystify The Poet, with a capital P. As the interview progresses, I notice Denise fidgeting, growing impatient. Is the interviewer asking the wrong questions? More likely, I think, she is impatient with answering the same questions others have asked, topics and themes she has moved on from. The interviewer wasn't aware that Denise has published a new collection of poems [*The Freeing of The Dust*] and so keeps asking questions about her previous books, *Footprints* and *To Stay Alive*. Her impatience leads Denise to anticipate the woman's questions before she has completely framed them, and, as often as not, I think that Denise mis-anticipates what would have been the thrust of the question. The French woman is nevertheless, very polite and doesn't exhibit any frustration when Denise takes off in a different direction with her answer.

"One cannot sustain 'lyric intensity' in a poem of considerable length; or, if one could, that quality we think of as 'lyric intensity' wouldn't remain the same throughout the poem. The reader would soon become numb to it." Denise is responding to questions about her long notebook poem that makes up most of her book *To Stay Alive*. The interviewer had spoken about its documentary qualities and had asked why some sections of the poem appear in verse while others are in prose.

"There have always been 'filler' sections between moments of lyric intensity in long poems," Denise explains, choosing her words carefully, while kneading the air with her hands. "Even in classical epic poems, even in Dante, there are filler sections that serve as bridges between the lyrical parts. But, whereas the poets of the past felt they needed to turn these connective passages into verse, that is, felt the need to versify their prose, modern poems, following the example of Williams's epic *Paterson*, for one, incorporate the actual prose.

"The modern long poem," Denise goes on, "is composed by a method very similar to collage painting. Juan Gris, would, for example, glue an actual bus ticket to his canvas when painting a Paris street scene instead of painting the ticket. Quoting from newspapers or from letters, from journals or from other prose, I didn't versify, that is, break into poetic lines the texts I was incorporating in my long poem unless I wanted to give the quotation emphasis. For example, I might break the prose into verse lines if I wanted to give the quoted text the same emphasis that I would were I reading it aloud to demonstrate a point to another person or to an audience."

Undated, Fall 1975

I looked in on Glover Circle today as D. had asked me to do while she is out of town on a brief teaching gig. All was well, but I noticed something familiar was missing from her study. I couldn't at first recall what it was though. On the bookstand that sits just inside the doorway, I realized that there was an empty place next to the framed photo of Doc Williams, seated in an armchair in some living room, perhaps his own, dressed in a white shirt, vest and tie. Everything else was in order. The portraits of Keats on top of the adjacent roll-top desk, the woodblock print in blue ink of William Morris's bearded face thumb-tacked to the wall just above the shelf.... Then I remembered there was a second photo of W. C. Williams, the same sized, framed. In the first one, W. C. W. is seated, staring back at the camera, his hands clapped together in applause or for emphasis in conversations. The missing one was a picture of Doc Williams in shirt-sleeves, rounding the corner of a shrub, striding across the manicured lawn of some college campus, the college chapel just behind him and to the left. "That photo was taken after he had had his first stroke," Denise said over my shoulder the first time I viewed it. "And just look at the vitality in his step!" She had added, "It's that kind of energy that allowed him to practice two very demanding professions." I wonder why she took it down from the shelf.

Undated Fragment 1975

The wife of a college professor cornered me during a dinner party in Worcester and quizzed me about Denise. She admitted to a fascination bordering on infatuation with her, whom she had met last year for the first time. The occasion was a poetry reading that Denise had given at the college where her husband taught English. During the reception that followed the reading this woman had gone up to Denise and told her how much she admired her as both a poet and outspoken anti-war critic. She told me she wrote a note to Denise afterward in which she revealed how much it meant to her to meet and talk with a person so unique and important. Then she pulled an envelope out of her purse and showed me Denise's reply. Denise had written back in a mildly scolding tone that she viewed her own life as being merely common, hardly distinguishable from any other. She was, Denise said, merely fortunate to be a medium for poetry, an instrument upon which the forces of poetry play. "Don't you feel that she is being overly humble," the woman asked, missing entirely Denise's peevish tone, which I interpreted as irritation at being fawned over.

December 24, 1975

Denise away at Yaddo, I stopped in at Glover Circle to check on things for her and to browse her William Morris books. She had left out for me on the desk in her study a manila envelope containing Xerox copies of her correspondence with William Carlos Williams. Unfortunately, I had errands to run this afternoon, so could only read quickly through the letters Williams sent her. I would have liked to have time to savor them, absorb their contents, and read them over again.

The first is a letter from W. C. W., dated November 1951, in reply to what I presume was a "fan" letter that Denise had sent him.

Admiration, he replied, makes one wish to better live up to the ideal of oneself the admirer has in mind, to do greater things, make greater efforts so that one feels more deserving of admiration in the future. But in the end, he says that he finds it impossible to do so and begs forgiveness of this admirer.

Already in the next letter from the same year, Williams invited Denise to visit him in Rutherford and commended her on poems she had sent him. The letters back and forth are pretty frequent from then on until about 1960 or 1961: invitations to visit, continuations of conversations begun when they had talked together face to face. I gather that Mitch always, or nearly always, accompanied Denise, making arrangements with Flossie beforehand; that speaking with W. C. W. was important to him, too (which I know was the case).

Williams' letters are filled with praise for Denise's poems, always noting her continuing growth as a poet. I get the sense that there is some quality in her work that he had never encountered before and which he was taking great trouble to define for himself. This mysterious something he likens to a subterranean power underlying her poems, something female (but not feminine). He at first finds it disturbing, but in time comes to accept and even delight in it. The combination she presents—an intelligent woman, a poet who plumbs depths, and a skillful craftsperson, among other things—are what he found unsettling at first. About her book *With Eyes at the Back of Our Heads* he wrote, "The words, the choice of words you use is disturbing to a man. It is linked to something unknown to the male wonderfully well used. As an independent artist you hold the key to the attack." Although he is not specific, I think he is pointing to the sensuous language of Denise's poems and her unabashed eroticism, which he found both disturbing and exciting. He says,

> there is something unrevealed in such writing ... something deeply buried. When it is a woman that is involved [in the writing] the mystery deepens, it is something cryptic which the world solves by calling her a whore. But the unresolved element of superlative artistic excellence, forces a reevaluation upon us.

Occasionally, he makes suggestions about improving a poem she has sent him, e.g., "cut that whole first line." Other times he points out when she is retreating to the English metrical line she displayed when he read her first poems, instead of utilizing the American speech rhythms and free-verse/organic form (although he doesn't use that term).

December 26, 1975

(Returned to read the letters in a more leisurely and thorough manner, but became so absorbed that I could not finish, so took the liberty to bring them home with me to read and return later.)

From the start, Denise professed to want to follow his example of experimenting with the American idiom and seeking a meter, a foot, evolved from it. Williams warns her that it is a hard road to follow, that she would be a lot easier on herself if she stayed with traditional metrics and followed instead the example of someone like Richard Wilbur, because doing so has the advantage of joining poets who belong to the literary establishment.

> You write well but you know what an advantage the poets who follow the academic patterns possess, even such relatively acceptable poets as Richard Wilbur with their regularly arranged lines, their rhymes and stanzaic forms possess. Do not underestimate it. The world they represent is not your world but it is a world that occupies the driver's seat.

W. C. W. seems to be testing her in this and other letters to gauge whether she just wants to superficially imitate him or whether she is truly looking to him as an example to follow in pursuing her own deepest need as a poet. Even after he is convinced that she is sincere, he continues to warn her of the difficulties she will face by striking out into uncharted waters. In one letter from 1957 he wrote:

> ... have never forgot how you came to me out of the formalism of English verse. At first as must have been inevitable although I welcomed you I was not completely convinced, after all, I wasn't completely convinced of my own position, I wanted you to convince ME.

He speaks with the voice of an innovator who was largely misunderstood and unappreciated by his peers, someone who has suffered hardships for his integrity. He always adds a note to remind Denise that writing is hard work but he encourages her to keep plugging away at it, suggesting that rewards will eventually come from doing it. "Cut and cut again whatever you write—while you leave by your art no trace of your cutting—and the final utterance will remain packed with what you have to say," is his advice to her in one letter. "But in the end, you must say whatever you have to say." And he adds, "without honesty completely outspoken you will not succeed in moving yourself or the world."

Williams tells her early on by way of encouragement to "write against all that may occur to stop you…. Writing always better and better, more pointedly, with your eyes wider and wider open." This is one of several letters in which Williams mentioned Sappho: "It may be that women are different than men in that, they may have to strip themselves barer than men do, the history of Sappho seems to indicate it—nothing held back." He obviously found something to admire in Sappho. In fact, he sent a published broadside to Denise of a Sappho fragment he had translated.

Did he just happen to be reading Sappho at the time when these letters were exchanged or was there something more intentional going on? Did he feel that an answer to the mystery Denise presented to him as a poet could be found in Sappho? That's the impression I get from the letters, although I don't know the context of the talk he and Denise had about Sappho when they were in each other's company.

I get the impression from these letters that for the first few years of their friendship, Denise was shy in his presence, seldom talking or offering an opinion. There is mention in one letter of Creeley also being present during her visit—maybe she and Mitch went to see Williams together with Creeley, who was after all Mitch's friend and classmate from Harvard. She mentions feeling out of place in the conversation conducted among men. Of course, many of Williams' visitors were ambitious young men, and perhaps Denise really was shy, or at least unaccustomed to the way men conversed. She mentions her insecurity and lack of confidence in her art. She contrasts herself with Creeley at one point, saying that she trusts too much to instinct and luck and doesn't feel that she *knows* what she is doing. She goes so far as to say, "I don't have an interesting mind."

I was shocked, reading this. The Denise I know is self-confident, outspoken, highly opinionated and articulate! I find it hard to believe but for the evidence in these letters that Denise could ever be intimidated by any man, or be afraid to open her mouth. Williams mentions in one letter that he is often perplexed and finds her inscrutable during visits, wondering what she is thinking, but then when he receives a batch of her new poems in the mail, he says that his questions are always answered and he is left somewhat astonished.

It was a striking contrast then to read the copy of a letter Denise sent him from about six years later (1960) when she resists Williams' attempt to enlist her in his campaign to championing the American idiom in poetry.

> You must take into consideration that I grew up not in an <u>American</u>, and not in an <u>English</u>, but a <u>European</u> atmosphere…. And then when I came to the U.S., I was already 24 years old—so tho' I was very impressionable, good melting-pot material, the American idiom is an acquired language for me.

She clarifies that she sees herself as an artist whose inheritance is European and not narrowly British in contrast to Williams' full-blown American position: "Certainly I am an American poet, if anything—I know I am not an English one—nevertheless I feel the great European poets 'belong to me' as an inheritance too." She tells him that she is a poet who sometimes writes in the American idiom but at other times reverts to the British diction of her childhood.

> And I believe fervently that the poet's first obligation is to his own voice—to find it and use it. And one's 'voice' does not speak only in the often slipshod imprecise vocabulary with which one buys the groceries but with all the resources of one's life whatever they may be, no matter whether they are 'American' or of other cultures, so long as they are truly one's own & not faked.

This is more like the Denise I know, the mature, self-confident, self-knowing artist who is aware of her uniqueness and resists the attempts of others to narrowly categorize her. Williams may have been disappointed by this reply but, apparently, he got what she was saying. Because in another letter he acknowledges her heritage as part "druidic" and part "Hebraic."

Over the years, I have talked with Denise about Williams and I have listened while she spoke about him to audiences at lectures and poetry readings, but those times she has always kept the focus on his work, its place in American poetry, and its value for poets of her generation and future poets. She seldom made anything more than a passing remark about her personal friendship, or gave details about her visits to 9 Ridge Road.

I do recall about two years ago that she mentioned having recently visited Flossie Williams and that had Flossie given her as a parting gift a pair of slippers, which Denise treasured. And recently, this past spring, I think, when she went to New York to meet with her publisher James Laughlin, upon her return she mentioned that together they had gone to Rutherford to visit Flossie. Denise didn't offer any details about that visit, just that they had done so. Then, this fall, talking one day about Robert Duncan, Denise had made a passing remark about once making a memorable visit together with Duncan to Williams. She stressed the word memorable, savoring the memory as she spoke.

One thing Denise did tell me with respect to this correspondence was that she regretted not writing down what transpired right after each visit to Rutherford. She complained that there were so many details she forgot because of her poor memory. (Poor memory is something we share, which is why I have taken it upon myself to keep this notebook record of my conversations with her.)

There is one letter to Denise in which Williams talks about Whitman. Evidently Denise had pointed Williams to a poem titled "This Compost," which she had "discovered" and thought to be one of Whitman's greatest short poems. Williams responded that he had been unaware of this poem and thanked Denise for pointing it out to him. He goes on the comment that, yes, the spirit of the age had touched

Whitman but that for all his profundity, he is nevertheless open to attack on formal grounds. He didn't invent anything usable. Look at the poets writing today, W. C. W. noted, reading their poems you couldn't tell that Whitman had ever existed. Strangely, Pound seemed to have come to an accommodation with the legacy of Whitman, moreso than Williams did. I'm thinking of Pound's poem "Pact." I would have thought it would be the other way around.

* * *

Denise told W. C. W. in a letter dated October, 1960, to write her in the future at a new address: 277 Greenwich St, #7. This is the very apartment that Sidney Goldfarb inherited from her and Mitch and where I crashed on Sidney's couch in 1971 or 1972 when I first went down to the Village for a week to check out the poetry scene and to play chess. [As a kid growing up in Buffalo, following Bobby Fisher's meteoric rise to the top of the chess world, I had read about the Manhattan and Marshall chess clubs and was eager to visit them.] I remember the flat had a cast iron claw-foot bathtub that stood in a corner of the kitchen, and that the toilet was in the hallway outside, shared with several other tenants on the same floor. Bob Hershon told me that Denise offered the *Hanging Loose* editors use of this apartment to collate the loose mimeographed pages of an early issue of the magazine—when it still "hung loose".

***

In one letter Denise mentions visiting Laughlin in NYC at his New Directions office and that he read to her Doc Williams' poem "Heel & Toe." She told W. C. W. that she danced an Irish jig right there in front of him as an expression of her exuberance for the poem. That's the Denise I know and love!

***

I was surprised to read her letter to Williams from Oaxaca (1957) in which she states that she doesn't find the Mexican painters interesting, excepting the printmakers. Yes, Posada, of course, we shared a love for his engravings and prints, but she knew Richard and I were big fans of the muralists, too—Rivera, Orozco, and Sequeiros. Denise seemed to share our enthusiasm for them when she met up with us in Mexico City two years ago. They were all Richard and I could talk about. She gave no hint then that they bored her as visual artists. Perhaps she is referring to more contemporary Mexican painters and not the great muralists.

She also mentions in this letter to W.C.W. moving into the household where her mother had been living on Calle Crespo in Oaxaca. This is the very same address where Richard and I visited her mother, two summers ago. Fifteen years later [1974], Beatrice was still living at this same address with the same Mexican family, having become their adopted *abuela*.

December 27, 1975

Evidently, Denise gave a talk about her friendship with Williams at the YMCA in New York City during the winter of 1966–67. In the same folder with the correspondence are her notes for it. They consist of an introductory paragraph describing how she first came to read his poems, mentioning the fan letter she wrote him about his work, which lead to an invitation to visit him in Rutherford.

> I first began to read W. C. W. in Paris in the winter of 1947–48. Although I knew right away this was a poetry of utmost importance for me, I had great difficulty at first understanding it. It was not until about a year later, when I had arrived in the United States for the first time and had settled into a tenement apartment in NY, that I really knew how it sounded, how its pace, its gait, its often broken and open-ended structures related directly not only to American speech but, more importantly, to the very pace and gait and structure of the American life I had begun to live.

Of course, I've heard her describe this delayed appreciation and understanding of William's poetry before both in person and in her published interviews. She says that it was several years after her move to NYC, "getting" his poems, and writing him a fan letter that she first met him. "After my first visit to him and Mrs. Williams," she says, "I returned many times over the years and between visits we exchanged letters until he became unable to type without extreme difficulty." If I have the chronology right, Doc Williams had already had one stroke by the time she first met him. Others soon followed, which also impaired his speech:

> The visits were always exhilarating to me, up to the very last one made 6 weeks before his death. He liked to have me read aloud my own poems and others to him. No matter how frail his health he never failed to focus with excitement, intuitive understanding and the shrewd judgment of a craftsman, on poetry, which was the very center of his life. Sometimes he would write to me the next day after I had been out to Rutherford, to continue the conversation.

Most of her talk consisted of excerpts from his letters interspersed with her commentary. She connected what he says in these selections to her perception of his work, which she illustrated with readings from his poems. She also read one of her own poems, written long after she had first met Williams and not explicitly about him, titled "In Memory of Pasternak" to illustrate how great artists and poets have the power to "extend one's vision (the reader's vision)—not substituting their vision for one's own but causing one to see what one would otherwise not have seen—is what great writers and artists share however different from each other...."

I have a vague recollection of reading this in published form somewhere, perhaps it's in *The Poet in the World*—will have to check; or is that tribute a different one but touching on the same themes?

December 30, 1975

When Denise had finished with her fall teaching responsibilities, she went off to Yaddo for two weeks to get some writing done before flying to Mexico to visit her mother, whose health continues to decline. She had mentioned to me one day before she left for Yaddo that she had recently been working on new poems, adding, "You know, I haven't written a new poem this entire fall!" She also mentioned that day her plan to work on a short memoir about her relationship with Robert Duncan. She had promised it as an introduction for a book on Duncan to be published in Australia.

Today, Steve and I were waiting to greet her upon her return from Yaddo. The kitchen looked like a florist's shop: tall irises in a vase from Steve, red and white carnations in another vase from Jean [one of D's student's, whom she'd let house-sit while she was away]. She didn't have much to say about her stay at Yaddo, other than that she had eaten well, as always. "I've got a bit of fat on me," she said, puffing out her cheeks. I told her I thought she looked healthy, robust.

We sat with her at the kitchen table, snacking on coffee, bread and brownies while Denise went through the enormous pile of mail that accumulated in her absence. As she sorted things—correspondence to be read and answered immediately, bills, junk mail, etc.—she passed to us anything she thought we might find of interest, such as literary magazines, or notes from friends. Finished with the mail, Denise brought out a notebook in which she had written her Duncan memoir longhand and handed it to Steve, saying that she would need him to type it up for her. Steve remarked on how neat and legible her handwriting was. Leafing through it, Denise noted that it was 61 pages long. "Sixty-one pages!" I remarked. "You gave me the impression before you left for Yaddo that this was going to be short." "Well, it *is* longhand," was her response. "It will be considerably shorter when typed. Besides, it's mostly quotations. I had to go through my correspondence with Duncan that goes back to 1964. I found it very interesting to reread his letters." I had expected that she would return with new poems, perhaps additions to her Homage to Pavese series, but she made no mention of new poems. I surmised that the Duncan memoir had consumed her time at Yaddo.

I told Denise that while she was away I had read the biography of William Morris [by E. P. Thomson], which I'd found fascinating and informative. I was interested in reading Morris's political writings now, so asked her if I might borrow her copy. Steve mentioned that he had finally finished *David Copperfield* after three months of reading it in dribs and drabs. "But did you enjoy it," Denise asked? "Very much," Steve replied. "Myself, I've been reading *Barnaby Rudge* and finding it delightful," Denise told us. "It's one of the few Dickens novels that I haven't read, or at least not since my mother read it aloud to me as a child, which I hardly remember."

"You know," she said, "I've always been aware that Dickens had a lot in common with some of the great 19th-century Russian novelists, but it wasn't until just now reading *Barnaby Rudge* that I realized that he had things in common with Tolstoy. There is, of course, the element of grotesquerie in Dickens, which has parallels in Gogol, and Dickens' influence on Dostoyevsky has long been acknowledged. Did you know," she added, "that Dostoyevsky visited London and afterward wrote a very gloomy sketch about the city, very Dickensian.... But Dickens's handling of the crowd scenes in *Barnaby Rudge*—you know it takes place during the Gordon Riots in London—I found reminiscent of Tolstoy's feeling for crowds and masses of people in *War and Peace*."

December 30, 1975

I borrowed the *Political Writings of William Morris* from Denise's library. Back in my apartment, I flipped through it, before settling in to read the book; in doing so I discovered, lodged between two pages, a letter, written in longhand, addressed to Denise. The letters' author was an Englishman, who thanked her for giving him her personal copy of one of Morris's "Penny Pamphlets," an original of one of the political tracts Morris published in the late years of the last century and sold at a penny a piece. More than just grateful, he was overwhelmed by her generosity. He wrote that *he* never would have given away *his* first edition of a Morris pamphlet! In return, he mentioned sending the gift of a postcard portrait of Morris. The very one, I'm sure, printed on blue cardstock, that is thumbtacked to the wall in Deni's study. It keeps company there with an etching of Keats and two photographs of William Carlos Williams. The rest of the man's letter was mostly indecipherable except for one passage. I inferred from the context that Denise had written this man a note that accompanied the gift of the pamphlet. In it she'd mentioned to him that she had had this pamphlet in her possession since she was 12 years old!

January 3, 1976

Denise tells me she did write one poem while working on her Duncan memoir at Yaddo, titled "The Emissary." [*Life in the Forest*] It was inspired by her encounters with one of the other guests at the colony whom she associates with Death—Death's emissary, hence the title. It begins, "Twice this woman for whom my unreasonable dislike / has turned to loathing." It's a disturbing poem. I tried to explain to Denise why I thought so after she shared it with me but found I was stumbling over my words. My thoughts about it were jumbled. As a poem, I don't think it is successful because the details she includes to illustrate why she felt that this real-life person was an embodiment of Death strike me as superficial. I thought it was my failure to "get it," when Denise had read the poem to me, combined with my loss for words to explain just what it was that I felt didn't work, but now that she has had Steve type it up and has given me a carbon to read, I have put my finger on the problem. It *tells* me but doesn't convincingly *show* me how or why. It's a leap to go from the woman's "cold hands," "pallid face," and the "chill she brings into rooms" to recognizing her as an emissary of Death. The associations are just too personal.

I also found the poem disturbing because it revealed to me a side of Denise I had never seen before. The encounter that prompted this poem was with another writer whom Denise obviously knew and apparently detested. She also resents the woman's success. Denise could tell that I thought she was being petty. Denise at first withheld naming the person who inspired this poem but then changed her mind. "I suppose I should tell you that it's Tillie Olson. Thank, God, she rarely appeared at meals," Denise said, adding: "I showed it to one other person at Yaddo who felt the same way about her as I do, and he said that I had accurately portrayed the pall she casts over every gathering."

I couldn't hide from Denise that I was shocked by her revelation. She asked whether learning this had lowered my estimation of her. I stammered something to the effect that "No, it was perfectly normal and human to have such visceral reactions to certain individuals." Denise felt the need to explain that is was not jealousy that accounted for her response to Olson. "I have never felt lacking for proper attention or praise for my poetry," she said; "Neither have I ever felt slighted or held back as a writer because I am a woman." But, she went on to explain, she felt that Tillie Olsen did not deserve the accolades and attention she had received. "She has made a career out of her silence as a writer," was how Denise put it. What particularly needled Denise was that Olson behaved toward her peers in a condescending way.

Denise knew that I had admired Olson's work. She also knew that as I searched for models of working-class writers whom I might emulate, Tillie Olson's stories, like those of Meridel LeSueur, were, I felt, that rare thing: writing for, about and *by* working class American authors. This, I'm sure, is why she hadn't wanted to reveal that Olson was the poem's inspiration.

I had met Tillie Olson only once, and it was a very quick encounter. The occasion was when Denise and I read together at UMass–Boston to an overflow auditorium of faculty and students. For me it was a thrilling moment to have such a strong positive response from the students in the audience, who were in large part from blue-collar Boston. As we made our way down the aisle to the exit, one of the people who greeted us was Tillie Olson, who it turned out was the school's writer in residence at the time. She made a nod in my direction and offered something like, "Nice poems."

I didn't know who she was until Denise introduced me to her. I didn't have the presence of mind then and there to tell her how pleased I was to finally meet her and how much I admired her work. She and Denise exchanged a few words and then we took our leave because we were scheduled to speak in an English lit class. Denise said nothing to me at the time to indicate her strong disliked for Olson. I had no sense at the time of any animosity between them, or even lack of cordiality. Silly me! Reflecting on that encounter now after reading Denise's poem makes me feel once again like a naïve rube.

January 9, 1976

"I am in general opposed, as you know, to segregating women from men, blacks from whites; opposed to one group isolating itself from the other when the problems needing to be solved can only be resolved by both parties working, struggling together. However, the women who came forth in the class I visited and who spoke out of their own experiences convinced me that there are exceptions to that rule."

Denise has just returned from a reading engagement in my hometown, Buffalo. While there she had visited Lillian Robinson's creative writing class. Lillian taught in the Humanities Program at MIT the same year that Denise was there and had taken part in demonstrations against Pentagon-sponsored research. The Women's Studies Department at SUNY Buffalo is under attack, Denise told me, for excluding men from enrolling in their classes.

"They spoke of their fear of vicious criticism from teachers and fellow students and placed great emphasis on needing the assurance of a non-competitive environment, one that they felt could only be achieved if men were excluded, before they could feel comfortable revealing themselves by sharing the manuscripts they had hidden in drawers or stuffed under mattresses."

I told Denise we had a similar struggle in the early days of The Group School around a discussion group for teenage girls led by two women teachers. There were lengthy heated discussions between students and students, teachers and teachers, and students and teachers about excluding males from participating in the group. Based on my observations of creative ferment that emerged from that group and the transformative effect it had on the young females' self-esteem and self-confidence, I concluded that valuable things could happen in such an environment that would not have occurred had men been involved.

"I still believe, though," Denise responded, "that such segregation must be done with the clear knowledge that eventually the two parties have to come together again and work toward a common solution of their problem."

***

Today Denise mentioned a young writer/publisher whom she had met in her recent travels, "He produces very nice books," she said, holding out for me to see several that he had given her. "Unfortunately," she added, curling her upper lip in distaste, "his own poetry is pretty awful. He does the kind of thing I simply detest. Here, let me show you." Thumbing through the pages of a collection of his own poetry: "Look," she said, he writes, 'I've bin', spelled, b-i-n, instead of b-e-e-n." After showing me several more examples, Denise snapped the book closed and spit out the words, "Yick! Pooh!" while doubling over, as if disgorging some morsel of food that she found bitterly distasteful. After she had regained her composure, she laughed self-consciously, and then spoke in a controlled voice, but with her upper lip still curled in disgust: "I can't stand it when literate people try to write as if they were illiterate.

January 12, 1976

(Notes on draft copy of Denise's "A Memoir of and Selection from the *Letters of Robert Duncan*") [Published as, "Some Duncan Letters—A Memoir and a Critical Tribute," New & Selected Essays, ND 1992]

D.'s Duncan memoir is so rich. Many of the things I've learned from her in conversation, by reading her essays on poetry collected in *The Poet in The World*, or by osmosis—just being in her presence—have their origins, I'm discovering, in the dialog she carried on with Duncan through correspondence. For example, her distinction between the poem that arrives as a gift, fully formed, needing little or no tinkering, versus the more common poems that one works and works at. I found that her discussion of these distinctions helped me to understand my own writing process and to avoid the mistake of forcing poems and recognize when they still needed time to percolate deep in my subconscious. It was helpful to discover that this wasn't something she always knew or acknowledged.

> I had experienced 'lucky accidents' and the coming of poems 'out of nowhere', yet I needed and was glad to get from him an aesthetic

rationale for such occurrences—reassurance to counter the 'Protestant ethic' that makes one afraid to admit even to oneself, the value of anything one seems not to have 'earned'.

There are two or three things I'm getting from reading the account of their correspondence. First, although Denise has told me a lot about her childhood in England, I didn't know a lot about her courtship and marriage, her emigration to the U.S. or her early years in New York. This memoir fills in some of those details. For example, D. writes that her introduction to Duncan's poetry came in 1948 (the year I was born) in Florence, Italy, where she and Mitch, recently married, were vacationing, getting ready to enter the U.S. She says that she came across a review of Duncan's collection *Heavenly City, Earthly City* by Muriel Rukeyser in *Poetry* magazine in the American Library there.

> These lines, and the whole review, so stirred me that I convinced myself no one in Florence needed that particular issue of *Poetry* more than I did, and I not only kept it, but when we left for Paris, took it with me.

I love to hear Denise retell the story of her epiphany about the American idiom when she first realized that "hot dog!" was an expression of excited approval and not just the name of a wiener, and she has often talked about how she couldn't hear the rhythms in William's poems until she was living in New York, surrounded by American speech, but until reading this memoir I didn't understand the degree of culture shock she experienced when she first came to the U.S. and her struggle to acquire the "American idiom" for her own poetry. She says that when she first arrived:

> ... I was too passive, disorganized, and overwhelmed by unrecognized 'culture-shock' ... to do anything so methodical as try to find his [Duncan's] book or books: so that when I did happen upon *Heavenly City, Earthly City* on the sale table outside the Phoenix Bookstore on

141

Cornelia St., just a few blocks from where I was living, it seemed an astonishing, fateful coincidence—as in a sense it was.

It's interesting to hear Denise describe the ways she adapted as a poet to her new environment and moved away from her more literary British influences:

> Now I was quickly, eagerly adapting to the new mode of speaking, because instinct told me that to survive and develop as a poet I had to; and Williams showed me the way, made me begin to appreciate the vivid and figurative language sometimes heard from ordinary present-day people, and the fact that even when vocabulary was impoverished there was some energy to be found in the here and now.

I'm finding in the memoir how important a role Duncan played as D's mentor, sounding board, and companion in her exploration of a life in poetry. Reading their correspondence has made me reflect on the importance of my friendship with Richard and how we have served each other in similar ways. In our case, because we didn't live on opposite coasts but rather in the same apartment, there isn't a paper trail of correspondence to show what we shared and learned from one another. Instead of writing letters we'd talk over endless cups of coffee at the Blue Parrot café in Harvard Square, getting away from our Centre Street apartment and housemates to share drafts of poems, discuss our ideas about poetry, our dreams and our aspirations. What she says about Duncan holds true for me about Richard:

> For years, no praise and approval from anyone else, however pleasant, could have reassured me until I had Robert's approval of a poem; and if I had that—as I almost always did—no blame from others could bother me.

Another thing I realize reading this memoir is that it is in essence her reflection on her own growth and development as a poet, mostly in parallel with Duncan's, but at times, especially toward the end, diverging from him. Which came first I wonder, the poems she has been writing lately with her young poet friends and protégés in mind, poems such "the Quality of Genius" and "Growth of a Poet," which had made her think about her own growth and development and the role Duncan played in that; or was it the other way around?

I see too that her ideas about a "community of poets" that she stressed in the MIT poetry workshop have their origins in her dialog with Duncan. "This concept ... is closely tied to his recognition of poetry ... as being a 'power' and not a set of 'counters' as he put it." This includes her ideas of poetry as a sacred trust and shared tradition, which one is inducted into as into a priesthood, and where competition and careerism have no place.

> If Poetry, the Art of Poetry, is a Mystery, and poets are the servers of that Mystery, they are bound together in fellowship under its Laws, obedient to its power. Those who do not recognize the Mystery suppose themselves Masters, not servants, and manipulate Poetry's power, splitting it into little counters, as gold is split into coins, and gaming with it; each must accumulate his own little heap of manipulative power-counters.... But within the Fellowship of the Mystery there is no hoarding of that Power of Poetry—and so-called borrowings are simply sharings of what poetry gives to its faithful servants.

"Fellowship of the Mystery" sounds a lot like Tolkien. I suppose this should come as no surprise because she has often talked about a love of fairy tales, legends, and romances as being something she and Duncan shared, George MacDonald, for example.

I have always thought of Denise as a moralist, something which I am not, and which makes me uncomfortable in some of her political poems when they say or imply how one "ought" to think or act. It's reassuring to know I wasn't wrong about this. Denise admits to her moralist stance in contrast to Duncan's libertarianism when discussing the different takes she and Duncan have on the roles of "honesty" in their poetry. The idea that a poet must have something to say and must find in his heart the need to write are two things Denise taught me from the very beginning when she had us read Rilke's *Letters to a Young Poet*, back at MIT.

> ... such 'inner need' is related to 'having something' at heart 'to say', and so to a high valuation of 'honesty'—and our argument would arise over Duncan's sense that what I called honesty, he (as a passionate anarchist or 'libertarian') sometimes regarded as a form of self-coercion, resulting in a misuse of the art we served. He saw a cluster, or alignment, that linked <u>convictions</u> with <u>preconceptions</u> and <u>honesty</u> with <u>'ought'</u>, while the cluster I saw linked <u>convictions</u> with <u>integrity</u> and <u>honesty</u> with <u>precision</u>.

One clarification I find very helpful is about Deni's essay on Organic Form and the meaning of the word "discovery." This is another instance where she points out the difference between her take and Duncan's— her Neo-Platonism versus his what?

> In the fall of 1965, commenting anew on my "Notes on Organic Form," which he had read in an earlier 'lecture' form, he quotes with enthusiasm: 'Whether an experience is in a linear sequence or a constellation raying out from and in to a central focus or axis ... discoverable only in the work, not before it'—but in that phrase I meant 'discoverable' quite precisely—i.e., not 'which <u>comes into being</u> only in the work' but which, though present in a dim unrecognized or <u>ungrasped</u> way, is only <u>experienced in any degree of fullness</u> in art's concreteness: The Word made Flesh concept given body in Language. One cannot 'discover' what is not there.

I can't begin to name all the things I'm learning from this memoir. There's a lot that I just don't get and will require more study, in part because I have not yet read as widely and deeply as Denise or Duncan. There are many references that go right by me. Other things I'm just beginning to grasp and will need to mull over and read again. An example of this is her discussion of the difference between imagination and fantasy. She says, "the active imagination illuminates common experience and not by mere memory, but by supplying new detail we recognize as authentic." By common experience she means "that which conforms to or expresses what we share as 'laws of Nature.'" That much is clear to me. But then she goes into depths that I don't entirely fathom:

> Hoffman's fantasies, known to me since childhood, had given me pleasure because they were 'romantic' in the vernacular sense (and my edition had attractive illustrations) but they did not illuminate experience, did not 'increase the sense of living, of being alive', to use Wallace Steven's phrase.... To me—then and now—any kind of 'sci-fi', any presentation of what does not partake of natural laws we all experience, such as gravity and mortality, is a work of imagination only if it is dealing symbolically with psychic truth, with soul-story, as myth, fairytale, and sometimes allegory, do.

Maybe after I have read Hoffman's tales, this distinction will make more sense to me.

January 30, 1976

"Both sad and rewarding," are the words Denise used to describe her experience rereading the letters that make up her more-than-fifteen-year correspondence and friendship with Robert Duncan. Although she didn't elaborate, I felt I understood why she felt these conflicting emotions after I had the opportunity to read the draft of her Duncan memoir.

"Rewarding," I imagine because to read again the very words exchanged over the long years of their friendship is almost to re-experience the exhilaration of reading them for the first time but now with the perspective of hindsight, knowing the trajectory of their relationship. Things written, which at first were of little significance are now revealed to be the germs of later developments in their friendship, both positive and negative. And certainly, for Denise, it must have been very rewarding to review her development into the mature artist she is today, which the correspondence chronicles.

Denise found it "sad" to read Duncan's letters again because, she told me, she found in them an inescapable sense of Duncan's growing preoccupation with his work. "Every artist or writer is preoccupied with his or her work," Denise said. "But the richness and depth of insight that was so meaningful to me in his early letters I found reading them now to be gradually replaced by minute descriptions of his making of individual poems. They are full of extraneous details: typography, and hassles with publishers. There is also a lack of awareness on his part that I or anyone else for that matter might find it of no major concern or interest to learn in great detail about his working habits on specific poems."

She also spoke of finding a growing indifference on his part to other people's reactions. Denise described it as a sort of "this is what I feel like revealing, now you take it or leave it." She added, "I have no doubt that Duncan is a genius, but he is not the warmest person. In fact, he can be quite cold and unapproachable."

I told Denise how much I liked the memoir. I found it rich with ideas, thought provoking, instructive. Reading it gave me a clearer picture of her own development as a poet. I also told her that I could see elements of my own ongoing development reflected in that mirror. Reading it had placed in perspective the importance to me of my friendship with both her and Richard. It helped me to see just how much I have learned both directly and by osmosis by being in her presence. In particular, it gave me the opportunity to reflect on the ways that our discussions of poems that I was working on had deepened my understanding of poetry; for example, the topic of how an artist should properly go about the work of revision, which has such a central place in the correspondence between her and Duncan. I also told her that the subject of poetry and the imagination that she has articulated so beautifully in her essays [in *The Poet in the World*], and which have been so meaningful to me, I found to be further clarified by reading the give-and-take between her and Duncan.

"Did you find the whole memoir to be too narrowly focused?" Denise asked me. "I tried to pick out and illustrate the dominant threads that run throughout our correspondence and that were at the core of our friendship. My fear is that someone reading it will be led to think that this is all there is to Duncan and the ideas we shared. Perhaps I need to include other aspects of Duncan's personality and mention some of the many other things and ideas in his letters to give a fuller picture of him?" I told her no, that I thought she succeeded in doing what she had set out to do. If she felt she needed to give a more rounded portrait of Duncan, then she would have to add an afterword. But, I said, I felt it was best left as is.

Undated fragment 1976

My becoming the father of a boy seems to have made Denise reflect upon her own parenting and on Nik as small child. "One becomes so attuned to the language children speak before they use real words that one begins to understand what they mean," Denise said today when I related that Andrai called a wash cloth "fwaff-fwaff." "Mitch and I kept a list of words that Nik coined—I have it saved somewhere," she said. "Of course, when they *do* begin to use real words, you quickly forget the invented ones they used to say." She continued, "I still remember one 'word' Nik used, "Tata-frilla;" it meant typewriter. Isn't it wonderful sounding, tata-frilla! It does sound like a typewriter typing, doesn't it! Tata-frilla! It's onomatopoeic!"

Undated fragment 1976

"Oh, look! It says here there are Spring Peepers," Denise exclaimed, looking up from the brochure that listed inhabitants of the wildlife sanctuary where we were walking. She read aloud as we strolled, "A woodland tree frog that is heard in the early spring calling with the familiar bird-like *peep*." She continued, "I listened to Spring Peepers all of one night recently, out the bedroom window of the house I was put up in when visiting Washington."

"Spring Peoples," she uttered after a thoughtful pause. "One summer at Putney, Vermont, where Nik was going to school. I passed a little boy in the woods carrying a jar of Spring Peepers." Denise hunched over her hands, cupped as if holding jar, imitating a child hiding something precious from the scrutiny of adults. "Whatcha got there," I asked him? She tucked he chin to her chest imitating the little boy, then, looking up sheepishly, said in a little boy's voice, "'Spring Peoples,' he said!" And she chuckled.

Undated, March 1976

Denise accompanied Jan and me—and baby Andrai in the backpack—on a Sunday walk at Great Meadows bird sanctuary, bordering the Concord River. The March sun had not yet cleared the ice from the two small ponds where in summer we see rafts of painted turtles. Whenever she is enjoying herself, as she was this afternoon, Denise speaks volubly without inhibition, liberally spicing her talk with anecdotes about her childhood, always taking great pleasure in the telling.

"*What* about peasants?" Jan, who had lingered at one of the ponds, asked, catching up to us. "Not peasants," I explained. "We were talking about pheasants."

"Peasants ... pheasants...," Denise repeated, then said: "that reminds me of...," as she launched into a tale from her childhood involving the teenage friend of her sister Olga. X (I don't recall her name), Olga's friend, Denise explained wanted to act in the movies. She hung around that section of London where movies were filmed, until eventually she did get a part as an extra. She got to play a peasant in a crowd scene from the movies titled *The Secret Spy*. When Olga's friend telephoned to inform her parents that she wouldn't be home in time for dinner because she had gotten a part in a movie, it was her little sister who answered the call. As Denise told it, barely able to contain giggles of delight, the girl's parents asked the little sister, "Who was that?" "Oh, that was X," the little sister replied. "She called to say that she won't be home for dinner because she is playing a pheasant in a movie called *The Secret Pie*."

Spring 1976

Denise was bursting with joy this morning after the poetry reading given by Judy [Katz-Levine, former MIT poetry class member] and Stevie [her secretary]. How to explain the exuberance she greeted me with when she opened her front door? I'm certain that I was the very first person she saw this morning. She was like a child who has been watching for weeks the robins in the eaves of the house outside her bedroom window, first building a nest, then attending to the eggs, watching all the while in agitated anticipation, and then literally bursting at the seams with excitement and joy to tell someone once she has heard the first peeps from the hatched chicks. Denise took my hand and pulled me through the front hallway into the kitchen where she was having breakfast, all the while dancing or skipping with excitement. "Didn't they read marvelously!" She exclaimed. "How they've grown in their writing!" They've really come into their own as poets!" Then she added pensively, "The things that young poets attempt and succeed at in their writing inspires me unlike anything in the work of my contemporaries anymore. When I listen to one of my contemporaries read their poems, I find I am saying to myself, 'I could do that just as well or better.' But listening to younger poets read, I don't feel competitive, but inspired. The things they try, neither I nor any of my contemporaries would think of."

Undated, spring 1976

Denise had just returned home from the West coast, where she had gone to lead a writing workshop. Sorting through the books, journals, and manuscripts she had accumulated during the week that she was away, she handed to me two books with the explanation that they were written by an Indian poet (from India), whose work she thought I might find of interest.

"He's a Sanskrit scholar who writes poetry in English, but who grew up speaking some obscure Bengali dialect, I think. Knowing Sanskrit, 'the mother of languages,' intimately, he claims that he can work comfortably in any of the other languages, which have their roots in it. However, he often makes mistakes in his poems which get in the way of the English reader's enjoyment—little inaccuracies, transpositions, and more often redundancies. He left me with the manuscript of his new book that is slated for publication in the fall. Although I told him that I very likely would not find the time to read it and comment before then,

I now feel that I must read it through and point out these inaccuracies which mar an otherwise good collection of poems before it goes to press."

"Here, look at this title," Denise said, pushing one of his books in my direction. "*Driftwood from the Seashore*. Of course, the seashore! Where else does one find driftwood. The title should simply be *Driftwood*. Time and again I am reminded," she continued, "what a tragedy it is for a writer to be spread across too many languages and never have a 'mother tongue' of one's own to write in."

February, 1976

I stopped by Glover Circle to visit Denise this afternoon just as I do most Sunday afternoons, but today I was more excited than usual because I had a new piece of writing to share with her. Last week I had left my book manuscript with her to read and comment on. [West End Press had previously published a chapbook (1974) of my work together with Richard Edelman's, with covert art by Nik Goodman. The manuscript I gave Denise to read was an expanded edition of that with new poems added. It was slated to be published by Sam Hamill's Copper Canyon Press as *The Buffalo Sequence* (1977), my first full collection.] I wasn't expecting her to critique the poems themselves, since she had seen them all before and we had already discussed each at length. Rather, I was seeking her input on the arrangement of the poems, on the book as whole. It is very important to me that it strike the reader as a unified book and not just a grab bag of poems. Toward that end, I began to write a preface to explain to readers my notions of it as a book. The result was something like a prose poem, which I titled "To Make a Book." The way it turned out surprised and pleased me and I wanted to share it with Denise right away.

Denise led me into the living room. She informed me that Nik, up from NYC visiting for a few days, was resting upstairs. I sat on the couch and she sat on the stuffed chair next to it, perched on the very edge of her seat, chin on palm, resting the weight of her elbow on the chair arm, offering me her full attention. She listened with eyes closed, rocking back and forth, savoring the words.

When I had finished reading, she cocked her head back, brought the circle she had made of her thumb and forefinger to her lips and with a smack of her lips pronounced, like a master chef savoring a dish, "Perfecto!" Her eyes seemed to sparkle with a childlike excitement. I was delighted to know that she considered it a success. "The first part," she said, "is really the prose poem, isn't it? The metaphor, the thing itself, moves always with a natural grace. It is only when we try to explain the metaphor that the words lose their ease and grace of movement and we become tongue-tied." She then pointed out where in the second part, a sentence needed reworking. "The second half," she noted, "is a commentary on the first in more pedestrian prose."

Then she went silent, closed her eyes, opened them and stared off into the distance. Before she spoke, she linked the first two fingers of her right hand with the two fingers of her left, as if links of a chain, and tugged as if to test the strength of the bond. "Do you recall the prose piece I wrote about Robert Duncan's early poems? It's in *The Poet in the World*. I feel that this piece of yours is a brother to it. They are each an essay in the form of a prose poem. In mine, I used the metaphor of climbing the lower slopes of Mount Blue, in Temple."

Later, when Nik joined us, Denise insisted that I read "To Make a Book" to him. He said afterward, he had also tried to write a description of the creative impulse and like me had used the metaphor of a stream that flows underground, a stream that one couldn't see but only sense, and like a dowser was able to find where it eventually bubbled up to the surface. But, he added, the idea of the creative impulse submerging and resurfacing again and again in a cyclical fashion had never occurred to him.

As the afternoon wore on, our conversation turned to my work teaching poetry to children in the Worcester Public Schools. I have found grade-school kids to be very observant of their surroundings in a strikingly sensual way. I told Denise that I had been using Reznikoff's poems in *By the Waters of Manhattan* as models to get the kids to describe the details of their environment just as they experience them. I mentioned that my approach seems to be in distinct contrast to that of Kenneth Koch who is very popular with teachers and who emphasizes,

151

"wishing," daydreaming, and fantasy. I have found, I explained, that the results of that approach lacked in substance, leading to fantasy rather than something truly imagined.

"I have just received a letter from Robert Bly," Denise interjected, "in which he complains about the same thing. He said that he is disturbed by the work of young writers he finds in a lot of literary journals today because they have a tendency to just daydream, nothing more profound than that." Denise went on, "It's ironic that Bly, of all people, should make such a remark when my objection to much of his own writing is that it feels to me little more than daydreams.

IV. ESTRANGEMENT

Our lives went through significant changes in the late 1970s. Denise resigned from Tufts after the English Department hired a new faculty member, despite her passionate opposition. Her reason: she felt his academic approach to poetry contrary to hers. Soon after, she began spending spring semesters on the West Coast, teaching writing at Stanford. Richard had married the young Mexican woman he'd met while we two had traveled the length of that country a few years earlier. I now had a child and was living with my toddler son and his mother. Responsibilities to our partners and families prevented the three of us from spending the kind of quality time together we had once enjoyed. Geography played a role, too, when Richard later moved back to his hometown, Milwaukee. My domestic arrangement abruptly ended about the same time. Soon after, I too left Cambridge to live with the Worcester writer Mary Bonina, whom I later married. Although we continued to visit one another, write letters and postcards, and share poems, the charmed period of our lives together as "musketeers" came to an end.

Small fissures had begun to appear in my relationship with Denise that I was largely oblivious to at the time, a result, I now see, of my new friendships in Boston, Worcester, and New York with poet peers outside Denise's immediate circle. It began innocently when John Crawford, editor of *West End* magazine, arrived in Boston in early 1973. Like other Movement activists new to Boston, John had been told to "look up Denise Levertov": she could put him in contact with people he might want to meet in the area. I was introduced to John in Denise's Glover Circle kitchen. I don't remember whether he had already relocated from Manhattan or was just then contemplating his move.

Unlike most others we knew and associated with, whose politics were "New" Left, emphasizing social issues such as abortion, feminism, gay rights, etc., John was in the "Old" Left camp, a proud card-carrying member of the Communist Party USA, which promoted class struggle. Given his youth, this admission surprised both Denise and me. But any hesitation I had about John's politics quickly evaporated when he spoke about his ambition to seek out and publish working-class writers. Having recently embraced my Polish, blue-collar Buffalo roots, I was won over.

John was a Columbia grad with a PhD in literature. Like many other Upper West Side students and alumni, he had hung out at the West End Bar, launching *West End* magazine from there. Four or five issues were already in print when he resettled in Boston. He soon enlisted me to help him identify Massachusetts poets with blue-collar family backgrounds. He also published a selection of my new poems in his next issue.

Another time when the two of us were visiting Glover Circle, John proposed a special issue of *West End* featuring two poetry chapbooks under the same cover, one by Richard, the other by me. Denise applauded this idea, feeling the two of us were ready to have a collection of poems in print, and she suggested John consider her son Nikolai to do the cover art. Nik, a talented artist who had studied at the Rhode Island School of Design, was at the time apprenticing with renowned print-maker and graphic artist Leonard Baskin. The result was the first publication of my entire *Buffalo Sequence* plus "Thoughts on Poetry," an essay on poetics John had commissioned me to write. Nik's black-on-white linoleum-block print of an urban skyline graced the front cover.

The next year I landed a job as poet-in-residence for the Worcester Public schools. A central Massachusetts blue-collar industrial city, Worcester was a lot like my hometown Buffalo. There I fell in with a group of young poets who had the working-class credentials John sought for a Massachusetts Poets issue of *West End*. A year or two later, when, in addition to the magazine, he began to regularly publish books, John enlisted my editorial help. Denise, however, didn't share my excitement. She expressed concern that editing books for John's press might distract from my own poetry. Neither did she welcome our creation of a worker-writers group, reviving Depression era proletarian models. It was another example of her dislike of poetry written for an audience, workers in this instance instead of women.

John made frequent trips back to Manhattan. On several occasions, he invited me along to share the driving. There, he introduced me to his Communist Party mentors, Lou Diskins, president of International Publishers, and culture editor of the *Daily World*, Adelaide Bean. A few years later, in 1978 and 1979 I joined John in Kansas City for two People's Culture conferences he'd helped organized, featuring such Depression-era proletarian writers as Jack Conroy and Meridel LeSueur, plus veterans of HUAC hearings Manny Fried, and Thomas McGrath. Although Denise never said a word about my fellow-traveling, I should have sensed a growing chill replacing her initial enthusiasm for my collaborations with John.

I thought Denise would be pleased to learn I had been invited to join Brooklyn-based *Hanging Loose* poetry magazine as an editor after Crawford moved West, resettling permanently in Albuquerque. Emmitt Jarrett, whom I replaced on the staff of *Hanging Loose*, had been a student of Denise's in New York in the mid-sixties. The other editors, Ron Schreiber, Robert Hershon and Dick Lourie, were all ten or more years older than me, and had all known Denise in New York. Dick, like Emmett, had also been a student of hers. From the magazine's inception in 1966, Denise served as contributing editor. Before I joined it, the pages of *Hanging Loose* was where several of my poems first appeared in print, in two special supplements compiled by Denise.

But despite these many connections, and despite her personal friendships with some of the editors, I learned that Denise had always had a contentious aesthetic relationship with them. She grew increasingly estranged from the editorial choices she found in the magazine's pages, eventually asking to have her name removed from the masthead as contributing editor a few years after I joined. Although always eclectic and national in scope, *Hanging Loose* published more writers from New York than anyplace else, including, by the time I came on board, some of the most prominent 2nd-generation New York School poets, such as Paul Violi, Tony Towle, and Charles North.

157

Although never overtly hostile to their poems, as she was toward Language Poetry, Denise never warmed to it either. I sensed she found it the insular work of a coterie. At first through subtle hints, then more and more explicitly, I picked up that Denise did not approve of my involvement with *Hanging Loose* or with the diverse influences its stable of writers began to have on my own poetry.

More significant, a personal rift subsequently emerged between us over the ways we each went about writing political poetry. From early on, I had followed Denise's lead, believing that writing about political subject matter was an important and valid thing to attempt in poetry, though difficult to do well. We both looked to the example of Neruda, whose statement she often cited, that "Political poetry is more deeply emotional than any other except love poetry."

But although I admired many of her Vietnam-era poems, such as "Life at War," and some of her later anti-nuke and cautionary environmentalist poems, I found the poems in which she expressed political anguish and moral outrage to be too didactic and preachy for my taste. In poetry, I believed, one should never lecture, hector, or brow-beat. My approach was more indirect, using irony to raise readers' awareness by pointing out contradictions and satirizing the pronouncements of politicians and public policy makers. Bertolt Brecht and Zbigniew Herbert were my models; at other times, I wrote poems of witness in a documentary mode after the examples of Ernesto Cardenal and Charles Reznikoff.

When my second poetry collection, *All the News*, appeared, I sent Denise a copy. Her response was hardly enthusiastic. "The Brechtian poems [in *All the News*]," she responded in a letter, "seem to me good of their kind—as you know, it's not a kind I especially like, i.e., I like more musical poetry, but this kind can be elegant too when it's precise—& can be useful in the way that Peter Maurin's 'Easy Essays' are." (Co-founder of the Catholic Worker Movement, Maurin expressed his philosophy through his "Easy Essays.") This struck me as damning with faint praise. She seemed to be implying that the poems were little better than agitprop.

Denise's response in 1993 to my next book was harsher and more direct: "I wish I could speak warmly of your new book, [*Special*

Handling] but as you know I have long felt you took a wrong turn poetically when you came under the influence of Brecht's least compelling, flattest poems, and I much regret the abandonment of (do you feel it abandoned you?) your lyrical strength." She went on to lecture and admonish me, "… poetry must sing, must dance, must defy paraphrase.… So I feel you have chosen all these years to produce some other form of writing and call it poetry. What you do, you do well. But it is not what I believe to be poetry." That stung.

Denise had permanently resettled in Seattle by then. I wanted to keep up a dialog; after all, she had profoundly influenced my life and career, but my attempts were rebuffed. Her replies to my letters were terse and unsatisfying, and eventually stopped. "This is not, I have to point out, the beginning of an ongoing correspondence," she made clear in her final letter, "because I'm making strenuous efforts to cut down on mail. I just can't cope with it any more.… And I hope you realize that this is an aesthetic judgment and not meant to be hurtful. It was a choice between saying this or not writing at all." But I was hurt and offended. Shortly after, I learned she was terminally ill with lymphoma.

Her silence left me alone to try to make sense of the erosion of our friendship and why it had come to such an unsatisfactory end. I never entirely believed her aesthetic rationales. Was it just disappointment, or had I given offense? Did she feel I had in some sense abandoned her for a wider literary community of my own making? Mitch, her former husband, with whom I remained friends, tried to be helpful, reminding me Denise could be "difficult:" principled, sometimes rigid, temperamental, easy to take offense, and prone to pick fights with poet friends and protégés—even, he pointed out, with their son, Nikolai.

Denise was the same age as my own mother, and I was just a year older than Nik, but I took small comfort in hearing about Denise's complicated, often strained relationship with him. Her strong opinions about how he conducted his personal and professional life as an adult, her "bossiness," led Nik to withdraw; he stopped speaking to her altogether for several years. But with Nik, who closed her down, Denise kept trying to reopen lines of communication. In contrast, she had closed me down. I was the one trying to reopen channels.

159

Denise's insistence that poetry must "sing" was a mantra, an aesthetic principle I'd heard her repeat often, but I also recalled that she could be selective regarding the poets to whom she applied it. In later years, the range of her criticism seemed to widen as when, for instance, she distanced herself from, Robert Creeley. She said she felt closer to the melodic late verse of Galway Kinnell than to Creeley's language play, formal invention, and syntactical dislocations—her *melopoeia* versus Creeley's *logopoeia*, was how she characterized it.

Similarly, she had once, in a *Nation* review, lavished praise on Robert Lax's early circus poems but encountering the poems of his later mature style, several of which appeared in *Hanging Loose*, she expressed disappointment that he had abandoned musicality for an abstract minimalism. Ironically, Creeley and Lax, both of whom I admired, were poets whose work Denise had introduced me to. Perhaps the "music" I still found in their poems was of a different kind than she had in mind: repetitive sounds, in Lax's case; speech cadences in Creeley's. I still favored Louis Zukovsky's inclusive formulation, one that Denise introduced me to early on, which held that poetry was an integral, in the mathematical sense, it's lower limit speech, its upper limit song. Poetry needn't only and always "sing."

I looked in vain for consolation in the examples of poets, once her friends, I knew she had picked fights with. Although I had applauded her break with the unnamed "genial poets" during the Vietnam War, I felt conflicted when she ended her friendship with Adrienne Rich, whom I continued to admire both for the power of her poems and the fierceness of her political commitment.

When, famously, Denise broke off all communication with Robert Duncan, whom I never knew personally, I took her side in their argument. However, reading much later the telephone book-size *The Letters of Robert Duncan and Denise Levertov*, which appeared years after both were dead, I discovered a side of Denise I hadn't previously taken stock of. Those letters opened my eyes to just how opinionated, intransigent, and aesthetically narrow she could be. "I had reserves," Duncan wrote to her in one early exchange (November 1967), revealing a side of her I hadn't known, "when you were explaining at the

Conference in Washington about your sense that the Concrete poem is wrong—even morally wrong ... one's morality must begin with the rule *no ought*...," Duncan had admonished her. "But you shld be reserved about deciding that some expression in art is 'wrong' when there is evidence everywhere of creative activity in said direction...."

Her stance—ethical? moral? or purely aesthetic? —and Duncan's response, resonated for me with her reaction to my Brecht-inspired poems, which she also called "wrong." But by then it was far too late to take this up with her.

In February of 1997, a call from Dick Lourie brought me the sad news that Mitch had died in Temple after a brief and painful bout with pancreatic cancer. Then in December, Richard Edelman, who kept in touch with her, called from Milwaukee to tell me Denise, our friend and mentor, age 74, was dead.

After hanging up the phone, I got into my car and drove across Cambridge to Somerville. Darkness had fallen. I parked under a streetlamp in the cul-de-sac, staring out at her old house. No. 4 Glover Circle looked unchanged, despite new owners: its exterior untouched, displaying the same two-toned shingling. I lost track of how long I sat there. My mind flooded with memories as I reflected on the decades of our friendship and our final falling-out.

Just shy of fifty, I was about the same age Denise had been when, long ago, I sat for the interview in her MIT office. I thought back to those first encounters during a period of national social unrest and widespread opposition to the Vietnam War. Lines from Wordsworth, a favorite of hers, came to mind about a similar long-ago time in his life of revolutionary ferment and hope for change: "Bliss was it in that dawn to be alive / But to be young was very heaven!"

I recalled my initial reaction to meeting Denise. Seated across from her in her office, she had set my nerve ends to tingling. She had seemed to emanate an aura of charged emotion when she spoke. That night, in dream, she had appeared as Kali, the Hindu goddess of death and destruction—"all-devouring" Kali: hair disheveled, eyes bloodshot, tongue lolling, wearing a garland of severed human heads. I had startled awake, I recalled, sweating. There was something unique

161

about this poet, Denise Levertov. She seemed to possess a kind of intelligence alien to my rational, scientific training, I had thought at the time; an intelligence more formidable for its distance from mine? I was determined to find out what that "something" was.

Now, seated in my car, that dream of Kali struck me as prescient, an apt representation of her and what she came to mean to my life. Not simply the wrathful destroyer but something more nuanced and complex. Despite her frightening form, Kali, I had since learned, was considered the kindest and most loving of Hindu goddesses, regarded by her devotees as the Mother of the whole universe, and was viewed as nurturer and protector as well as destroyer. "Bingo," I realized for the first time, "those dual aspects *were* Denise!" I couldn't hold back my tears.

Acknowledgments

I am grateful to the many people who offered advice and encouraged me to complete this memoir:

♦ Fellow MIT wordsmiths Richard Edelman, Margo Taft Stever, Don Krieger, Ernie Brooks, Lucy Marx, Judy & Barry Katz-Levine, Paul Callahan, and Arthur Sze;

♦ The writer friends whose interest spurred me on: Michael Basinski, Henry Braun, Barbara Gates, Sandy Gregor, DeWitt Henry, Bob Kimber, Charles North, Michael True, Tino Villanueva, and Jessamyn Wolff;

♦ Levertov's literary executor Paul Lacy, and her New Directions Press editor Barbara Epler;

♦ Christina Davis, Curator of the Woodbury Poetry Room at the Lamont Library, who assisted me in locating the recording of a Levertov poetry reading at the Harvard Divinity School circa 1973;

♦ The editors who published several chapters of this memoir in early versions: my *Hanging Loose* co-editors Donna Brook, Robert Hershon, and Ron Schreiber; Kevin Gallagher (*Jacket* and *SpoKe*); Askold Melnyczuk (*Arrowsmith Journal*); Joseph Torra (*Let The Bucket Down*) and Sandra Tyler (*The Woven Tale*).

♦ I owe a special debt of gratitude Donna Krolik Hollenberg, who included a chapter in her anthology *Denise Levertov in Company* (University of South Carolina Press), and without whose council, editorial suggestions, and confidence in this project it would never have been completed; and to my "go to" editor in all things literary, Dick Lourie.

♦ And not least, I'm grateful to my spouse of almost four decades, the writer Mary Bonina. Mary had been a student in a seminar Denise taught at Assumption College in Worcester, Massachusetts, the summer before I took up my position as Poet-in-Residence for the Worcester public schools. "You should look her up," Denise sagely advised. "I think you'll find you two have a lot in common."

About the Author

MARK PAWLAK is the author of nine poetry collections and the editor of six anthologies; most recent *Reconnaissance: New and Selected Poems and Poetic Journals* (2016). Pawlak's poems and prose has been translated into German, Japanese, Spanish, and Polish, and has been performed at Teatre Polski in Warsaw. For the past forty years, Pawlak has been a co-editor of the Brooklyn, New York-based poetry journal and literary press Hanging Loose. To support his writing habits, he teaches mathematics at the University of Massachusetts Boston. He lives in Cambridge.